"Anyone who has ever played or c paid close attention to the third-t game will appreciate the author's history of diamond sign languag teller, and his latest book is a wel canon of baseball literature."

—*Booklist*

"No discussion of signs would be complete without those used in baseball, which are the subject of Paul Dickson's *The Hidden Language of Baseball*, a charming celebration of the role of cheating in our national game."

—DAVID L. ULIN, *Los Angeles Times*

"A swell diversion, full of little stories such as Bill Veeck's using telescopes to steal signs (and perhaps the pennant). We don't think you get enough of that nowadays. Dickson traces the secret art from its humble beginnings during the Civil War (where they were an extension of battlefield signals) on up to [the 2002] playoffs, when St. Louis snuffed out the Johnson/Schilling tandem, perhaps because of tipped pitches. While it doesn't decode the cryptics on the field today, *The Hidden Language of Baseball* offers up a little dessert buffet of anecdotes that should keep the fathers of America feeling tender and warm in their easy chairs."

—*Mudville Magazine: The Voice of Baseball*

"Hard-core fans will relish this lively and informative inside look at signs and sign-stealing. It gives a history and discusses the myths of the signs."

—*Sporting News*

"In this quick but sweeping examination, baseball historian Dickson explores the intricacies of baseball's 'hidden language,' the rapid-fire signs that are delivered in a manner that can escape even well-tutored fans. . . . Belongs in all baseball collections."

—R. C. COTTRELL, *Library Journal*

"An old-fashioned whiz-bang. . . . Dickson's most rewarding book yet."

—JAMES H. BREADY, *Baltimore Sun*

"Dickson's book contains enough inside information to dazzle even Tim McCarver and Al Leiter."

—*Legal Times*

THE HIDDEN LANGUAGE
of Baseball

PUBLISHED WITH SUPPORT FROM

Figure Foundation

SIGNING LANGUAGE

THE HIDDEN LANGUAGE

of Baseball

How Signs and Sign-Stealing
Have Influenced the Course
of Our National Pastime

| *Second Edition* | PAUL DICKSON |

University of Nebraska Press | Lincoln

Library of Congress Cataloging-in-Publication Data
Names: Dickson, Paul, author.
Title: The hidden language of baseball: how signs
and sign-stealing have influenced the course of our
national pastime / Paul Dickson.
Description: Second Edition. | Lincoln: University
of Nebraska Press, [2019] | Previous edition: 2003. |
Includes bibliographical references and index.
Identifiers: LCCN 2019005311
ISBN 9781496214638 (paper: alk. paper)
ISBN 9781496217851 (epub)
ISBN 9781496217868 (mobi)
ISBN 9781496217875 (pdf)
Subjects: LCSH: Baseball signs and signals—United
States—History.
Classification: LCC GV875.8 .D53 2019 |
DDC 796.357—dc23 LC record available
at https://lccn.loc.gov/2019005311

Set in Minion Pro by E. Cuddy.

Cleveland was playing Chicago. [White Sox] Runners were on first and third. [The Indians'] Schalk signaled to the moundsman for a curve. Speaker saw the signal flashed and ordered a delayed double steal. Gleason caught that signal, the White Sox switched positions and Schalk signaled for a pitch-out.

The pitchout signal was caught by Uhle, who was coaching, and Speaker signaled for a change. The result was that the runners held their bases and the pitcher wasted a ball. Schalk signaled again, the infield changed and Speaker ordered a delayed steal. Ray was warned and ordered another pitch out, but no sooner had he flashed that signal than Speaker had ordered another wait and Schalk, thinking to outguess Tris, ordered a fast ball. As Schalk changed his signals Speaker, guessing that he would do exactly that, signaled for the hit-and-run, with the result that a hit whipped through the infield, winning the game.

—BILL WAMBSGANSS describing the greatest play he had ever witnessed for the *New York Evening Post*; reprinted in *Collier's*, August 2, 1924, under the heading "Brainwork on the Diamond"

CONTENTS

PREFACE TO THE SECOND EDITION

The original version of this book was published in 2003 and went out of print in 2017. This new edition updates the earlier edition and contains a full account of the now infamous Apple Watch sign-stealing incident of 2017 and its impact on the future of the game. I would like to thank Rob Taylor and the University of Nebraska Press for agreeing to publish this book in a new edition.

I was born on July 30, 1939, in Yonkers, New York. My neighborhood in South Yonkers, a few blocks out of the Bronx, was then, is now, and will probably always be Yankee territory. My first full month on Earth was Joe DiMaggio's best month in pinstripes: between August 1 and September 1, he batted .405, with fourteen home runs and fifty-two runs batted in (RBIs). There were ten games alone in which he produced three or more runs. At about this time Yankee broadcaster Arch McDonald—with an eye on the sleek, new forty-one-ton Pan-American Airlines intercontinental Clipper aircraft—gave DiMaggio his most enduring nickname.

By the time I turned six, I knew that one of the reasons to end World War II was to put the Yankee Clipper back on the field. Another was to bring my uncles back to Bayley Avenue in South Yonkers. In those days four generations of my mother's family inhabited part of 5, all of 19, and all of 31 Bayley Avenue, which was my house. My great-grandfather Phil Lehrbach, who lived at number 5, was a fanatical Dodgers fan, stemming in part from the fact that he had been a business partner of Charles Ebbets in the 1880s: they were among the first to promote and profit from the immigrant sport of bowling, and under the leadership of a jovial restaurateur and great bowler named Joe Thum, they formed the American Bowling Congress in 1895.

In September 1944 my uncle George came home unexpectedly from the South Pacific for a few days of shore leave, and he chose to spend one of them taking me, his adoring five-year-old nephew, to Yankee Stadium. We boarded the old Hudson River Day Liner in Yonkers, chugged downriver, and got off in the Bronx, where we grabbed a cab to the stadium. We arrived very early, as my uncle was a devotee of batting practice.

He was in uniform with a chestful of campaign ribbons and the arm patch that identified him as a Seabee, a member of a navy construction battalion, which, among other things, boarded damaged, often burning, and sometimes sinking ships and tried to repair them. In the late summer of 1944 a decorated sailor at the ballpark was a rarity, and the man at the booth waved us through the turnstiles with a wink and without charge. An usher took us to the Yankee clubhouse, where a few of the players were lingering and where Tommy "Old Reliable" Henrich was holding court. Henrich, who had come up with the Yankees in 1937 and had been a major factor in the 1941 Yankee World Series championship, was in the uniform of the Coast Guard and, like his teammate DiMaggio, out of the lineup for the duration of the war.

Henrich immediately took us under his wing and got us seated in the owner's box, where we were fed by vendors who refused to accept payment and fans came by for Henrich's autograph. Positioned between these two great men in blue uniforms, I felt like an Arabian boy prince one might have seen in newsreel films.

This was, of course, exactly how I thought life should be led, and leaving the park that day I decided that I loved baseball. It would be several years before I understood that this outing was not typical, though it remains vivid for me to this day and allows me to believe that there are, in fact, perfect moments in an imperfect universe.

Both my uncles came back from the war safely, and DiMaggio and Henrich quickly reclaimed their positions, respectively, from the less than legendary Tuck Stainback and Bud Metheny. In the months after the war, my great-grandfather, then in his eighties, taught me all he could about the game while we sat in his stuffy one-room apartment under photos of himself with Lou Gehrig, Jimmy Foxx, Babe Ruth, and others. The Dodgers were his team, but he could not get DiMaggio out of his head and talked about him incessantly.

Listening to this immigrant who was almost eighty years my senior was akin to attending a baseball elementary school. My friends all knew what a home run was, but because of my great-grandfather I could tell them that not all home runs were equal and that a right-field pop fly in Yankee Stadium would be a home run at the Polo Grounds. He explained that there was a "short porch" at the Polo Grounds that made it easier for Mel Ott to hit more than five hundred home runs.[1] He argued that if Lou Gehrig had played at the Polo Grounds, he would have hit many more home runs. To this day when entering a ballpark for the first time, I take a look at the outfield distances and remind myself that all playing fields were not created equal.

He taught me about batters' distinct stances and grips (demonstrating with a rolled-up newspaper), showed me the fingering and delivery for different pitches, and so much more. One day he pointed to an article in the paper in which some professor somewhere claimed that the curveball did not curve at all but was an optical illusion. This occasioned an impromptu seminar on the behavior of objects in motion from a man who had spent much of his life performing magic with a bowling ball.

It took me a while to figure out one of my great-grandfather's best baseball lessons: that there is an inner complexity to the game not readily apparent to those in the ballpark or those who watch on television. And there is no better reflection of baseball's inner workings than the rich, largely unspoken sign language that has guided the course of games for almost 150 years. I would argue that it is one of the elements that most distinguishes baseball from other sports.

Even the most knowledgeable fan in the stands will never be able to completely decode a game, for many signs can never be seen by spectators and those that can are often given at blinding speed. But knowing who is giving signals, and under what circumstances, will heighten your appreciation of baseball as a game of silent strategy and precise coordination. It will also allow you to more accurately anticipate what will happen next, turning you from a spectator into a baseball insider, making you think like a catcher.

Former player, coach, and manager Wes Westrum once said, "Baseball is like church; many attend but few understand." One level of understanding comes when one realizes that managers, coaches, and players watch a game with an entirely different set of eyes than the fan in the stands—or even radio and television sportscasters. This book is your ticket to the game within the game, which is usually under way before the first ball goes into play.

Before a baseball game can begin, two things must happen: the plate umpire must signal "Play ball," and the catcher must give the pitcher a sign ordering the type and location of the first pitch. More often than not, these are finger signs delivered from the catcher's inner thigh. If the pitcher is uneasy with the pitch, he will "shake it off," vetoing it with a shake of his head or by some other gesture.

The catcher gives a new sign . . . or does he?

Maybe that "shake-off" was a decoy signal to the leadoff batter, intended to give him the feeling that there is uncertainty as to how he should be pitched or that the battery (pitcher and catcher) is off to a shaky start. The battery wants to establish its ability to control the leadoff batter—break his concentration—

and set the tone for the rest of the inning. A leadoff hit, especially on the first pitch, is to be avoided at all costs.

The batter may now call a quick "time-out"—dutifully signaled by the umpire—to remove dust from his eyes, which may actually be a ruse to let him step back and get an idea where the catcher is setting up for the first pitch or simply to upset the timing of the battery. The catcher may now call for another pitch—perhaps an inside pitch to warn the batter that sneaking a look back with a bogus time-out will not be tolerated. Meanwhile, when the final pitch selection is made, a middle infielder will get the message and relay that word to the rest of his team, perhaps thumping his mitt twice to let the man in right field know that the pitch is a fast ball to a right-handed batter, which, if it is swung on late, will send the batted ball in his direction.

The first ball has not been pitched, but the "head game" is already well under way. If one is counting the signals on one's fingers, one is now on the second hand and prepared to go to the toes.

THE HIDDEN LANGUAGE
of Baseball

Introduction

Secrecy, Deception, and the National Pastime

Over the course of nine innings hundreds of silent signs and signals are given and received—a thousand or more, excluding umpire signals, is a common estimate. Many will be false signals meant to mislead, others will carry routine instructions, and a few may spell out the difference between winning and losing. Most of these signs are conscious and covert, but sometimes an inadvertent sign in the form of an unconscious gesture or mannerism will tell what is to come. The ability to read the nature of the next pitch from a pitcher or catcher by a "tip-off" is one of the game's most highly valued skills.

Baseball's history is rich with gimmicky, sign-stealing schemes, but today it is a pure art based on the ability to read tip-offs and the ingenious decoding of an opponent's signs as they are being transmitted.

The art of giving, receiving, and protecting signs is crucial to the game of baseball. Signs and signals are the central nervous system that allows a ball club to function as a team both offensively and defensively. "Giving, getting and carrying out signs win close games," Hall of Fame player-manager Joe Cronin declared unequivocally.

Without these signs and signals—without some means of communicating with players in the field—a manager's influence over game strategy would be limited to what he could tell players when they are within whispering distance. "Signals are important," the late guru of the game Branch Rickey once said. "A manager who doesn't have control of his hitters and is unable to change a situation when he wants to doesn't have control of the game."

Without signs, catchers would become receivers only, while pitchers, hitters, and base runners would be largely on their own, and errors and miscues would proliferate. Offensive play would lose its elements of cohesion and carefully calculated risk, as all of the elements of strategy and surprise—steal attempts, bunts and squeeze plays, the hit-and-run, the run-and-hit, and the rare double steal—would become accidental ad-libs. By the same token the defense would be unable to set itself for different game situations, and pitchers and catchers would be unable to communicate.

The umpiring crew—the third team on the field—uses overt signs to make calls and govern the game: the clenched right fist and short hammered motion to announce that a runner is out, the palms-down gesture to proclaim a runner safe, the jerked thumb and arm motion for ejection (literally to "get the thumb"), and the various personalized motions announcing strikes. How would anyone be sure that the infield-fly rule had actually been invoked without the umpire punctuating the air with his clenched right fist raised straight overhead and his index finger pointing to the sky?

Much less obviously, umpires use covert signs to communicate with each other. For instance, if a manager storms out of the dugout to dispute a particular call, the other members of the crew will move toward the umpire being addressed. If the conversation turns to confrontation, the umpire in the firing line may choose not to immediately toss the aggressor out of the game but to give a "help" sign—commonly placing two hands on his waist—and another umpire will step in. This allows the confronted umpire to immediately walk away from the area and for the intervening ump to calm things down and let the manager know that this is his final chance to bring himself under control.

During the course of any game messages dart busily between managers and coaches, between coaches and hitters, between infielders and outfielders, between base runners and hitters, between catchers and pitchers, and between umpires. At any given moment, four or five messages may be crisscrossing an infield—twice or three times that many if a squeeze bunt is being called for. What the fan sees is an offensive play in which the man on third sprints with the pitch and the batter bunts the ball into fair territory, placing it so that the fielder cannot throw the man out at the plate. It is a beautiful and aptly named play that never ceases to appeal to the fans, but most will have no idea of the strategic maneuvering by which it is set up. What they may not know is that a lot of signs have to be transmitted to make it work.

Assume there are runners on second and third with no outs in the eighth inning of a tie game. The batter is a good contact hitter with little power. The manager or his dugout coach signals the squeeze play to the third base coach, who, in turn, signals the men on base and the batter, but because the opposition is trying to interpret, or steal, the sign, a number of decoy signals are also thrown. The runners signal back to the third base coach that they understand, and the batter acknowledges his assignment. These acknowledgments, or answers, may be as simple as touching the bill of a cap or brushing his hand across the letters on his shirt. If it appears that the batter has missed the sign, or if he signals that he is confused, the third base coach will repeat it or kill the play with a special sign.

Even if the sign has not been stolen, the defense will certainly suspect a squeeze play and has several defensive options, ranging from a pitchout to moving the infielders at the corners in to try for the play at the plate—either of which requires a series of signs and confirmations. The runner on second will be trying to steal the catcher's sign to the pitcher, which means that the catcher will also be trying to disguise his signs and bury the real one in a series of dummies. Once the pitch is determined, the shortstop or second baseman will signal that pitch behind his back to the outfielders so they know what to anticipate. An umpire suspecting a bunt play will signal the rest of the crew that a close play may be at hand. The catcher signals the pitcher, who acknowledges the pitch, and the ball is thrown. The batter squares around to bunt but fouls it off for strike one. The attempt to bunt now known, the manager may signal his batter the option of bunting or hitting away, starting the cycle over again.

Different situations demand different sets of signals. With a man on first, the shortstop and second baseman will exchange signals to determine who will cover second in case a steal or bunt is attempted. This signal must then be relayed to the catcher so that he knows who will receive his throw. The pitcher and the rest of the infield must be notified as well. A pick-off play usually called by the catcher is equally complex. The catcher must first indicate to his teammates to what base he is planning to throw, confirm who is going to cover that base, and make sure that the pitcher throws an outside fastball to facilitate the throw. The signal to start this play may be as simple as the catcher resting his mitt in front of his left knee with the back of the glove pointing to the base at which he plans the pickoff. But before he can attempt the play, he needs signals telling him that the infield is prepared. Needless to say, the opposing coaches and base runners are doing all they can to spot such signs.

Nothing in all of this is certain. A team in the field that assumes offensive signals are coming from a third base coach will have no inkling when the signs have been rerouted through the first base coach or a trainer, who may be signaling with a wooden tongue depressor with which he is cleaning dirt from his spikes—a move attributed to Tony LaRussa when he managed in Oakland. Defensive signs are anywhere and everywhere as players are moved and assignments are made. On the other side a pitcher may be getting finger signs from a catcher that seem overt and simple but must be added to numbers on the scoreboard before they can be decoded.

Sometimes base runners initiate signals. A runner who thinks he can steal second but doesn't have a "green light" to go on his own may query the third base coach, who in turn may query the manager in the dugout, whose signal is passed back through the coach to the player. The query may be as simple as the base runner dragging the back of his open hand across his mouth and the green light nothing more complicated than the coach taking a step backward.

Runners on second base attempt to read the catcher's signs and relay them to the batter. Hall of Famer Ozzie Smith once said, "It is more important to know the location of the pitch than the type of pitch," so the man on second is looking for not only the catcher's signal but how he is setting up as well. It is his job to get as much information to the batter quickly and subtly, indistinguishable from the natural fidgeting of a man on base. A shuffle of his feet may mean he does not have the sign, while putting his left foot over his right may mean he does. If he recognizes the sign for a fastball, he may touch his left wrist with his right hand, while letting his hands hang down for a curve. He may position his shoulders, perhaps dipping one slightly, to indicate position.

Because teams routinely try to steal each other's signs and signals, coaches and managers communicate in a form of code with real signs embedded in a string of false signals created to throw the other team off. The third base coach moving around like a man fighting off a swarm of gnats is disguising the real sign amid a flurry of bogus ones. Sometimes the whole presentation is a charade, a series of signs signifying nothing, designed only to confuse the opposition: the coach may have no message for the batter, or he may be pantomiming while the real signal comes from the dugout or the first base coach. Then again the play may have been set before the batter reached the on-deck circle, and everything seen by the defense and the fans is a decoy.

Typically, a set of signs from the third base coach will include not only a series of decoys—"dekes" to those on the field—but also an indicator and a hot sign. The indicator sets up the hot sign. For instance, the indicator may be putting the left hand on the right knee, and the hot sign for a bunt may be a cap tap. These are the only signs that matter and will be embedded inside a series of tummy rubs, arm crossings, nose flicks, forearm taps, sleeve tugs, and just about anything else that a coach can think of. Manager and pitching coach Ray Miller once observed, "Sometimes it looks like five guys trying to bring a jet onto an aircraft carrier. Some are signs. Some are decoys, and it's fascinating to sit there and watch the stuff flying all over the place." The third base coach's gestures are also one of the game's most easily mimicked elements, as demonstrated for many decades by baseball's clown prince, the late Max Patkin, or more recently by the late comedian Robin Williams in Anaheim during the 2002 World Series.

Teams work hard to keep their signs as cryptic and confusing to the opposition as possible. Jerry Narron, while third base coach for the Texas Rangers, kept his signs simple but had a different set for each player. In his early days as manager of the Cleveland Indians, Lou Boudreau had a system by which the same set of signals had different meanings for each third of the batting order. Preston Gomez, who also used different signs for each player when he was the third base coach for the Dodgers, said he didn't worry about a player being traded and carrying away knowledge of twenty-five different sets of signs. Gomez was also a master at stealing signs who taught others. In early 2018 Joe Maddon, manager of the Chicago Cubs, admitted that he had become an expert stealer of signs as one of Gomez's students in the arcane art.[1]

Casey Stengel was once asked what would happen if he found out that another team decoded his systems. "I ain't gonna change our signs," the "Old Perfessor" said. "I'm just gonna change what they mean." However, as was often the case with "Stengelese," even his own players were challenged by Stengel's signals. Frank Skaff, who was third baseman for the Brooklyn Dodgers in 1935 when Stengel managed there, later recalled his instructions for that season: "I'm looking at you, you're hitting. . . . If I'm walking away from you and spitting, you're hitting. . . . If I'm looking at you and spitting, you're NOT hitting. . . . If I'm walking away and not spitting you're NOT hitting." Later, when manager of the New York Yankees, Stengel jokingly announced, "I've got an ironclad system of signs. The other team can't steal 'em—and my fellows don't understand them!"[2]

Branch Rickey once observed, "If you want to steal signals the best and most important thing is to find the source of signals," and a primary deception is concealing that source.[3] Ed Michaels, a baseball commentator and broadcaster based in Florida, recalled his days playing for Delhi in the Delaware-Sullivan League in New York's Catskills when a man named Fred Ferguson was the manager. "Three signals were all that Fred needed. He never got out of the dugout. He sat there with a glove and a bat next to him, and he signaled a bunt when he picked up the bat, a steal when he picked up the glove and sat it on his lap, and a hit-and-run when he moved both the bat and glove. Meanwhile, the third base coach was going through all sorts of fancy gyrations which meant nothing. Nobody ever caught on."

Managers have used various simple devices to pass along real signals. Connie Mack's favorite instrument was a scorecard, which was always in his hand. According to Negro League historian John Holway, Rube Foster, who founded the Negro National League (NL) in 1920, gave signals with his meerschaum pipe when he managed the Chicago American Giants, and with this as his managerial baton he pioneered the triple steal and the hit-and-run bunt.

For the thirteen years during which Major League manager Bobby Winkles coached at Arizona State, the third base coach had but one meaningful sign—the "take sign," telling a batter not to swing—while the rest were meaningless. All the other calls came from the dugout as different players were told to stand up: A man whose last name began with *B* stood up for the bunt, a player whose name began with *H* signaled a hit-and-run, while an *S* man stood up for a steal. Winkles told Melvin Durslag in a 1979 interview that nobody ever caught on, as players in the dugout habitually mill around during an inning. However, the designated *B*, *H*, and *S* men were never to leave the dugout for the bathroom while Arizona State was at bat.[4]

If the colorful and often photogenic gyrations of the coach are key to a team's offense, the signals that are transmitted between catcher and pitcher are at the heart of the defensive game. Baseball historian Bill James has concluded that the reason catchers began to squat rather than crouch—as they used to do well into the twentieth century—was to hide signs from the opposition.[5]

At the heart of the battle between pitcher and batter is the simple premise that if the batter—even one of average talent—knows what pitch is coming, he has a much better chance of hitting it. The pitcher's advantage rises with his ability to mix pitches and keep the batter guessing. The best catchers develop a pattern of pitches for each batter and direct games with such skill that a pitcher will seldom decline their suggestions. In August 1967 Elston Howard was traded to Boston and helped the Red Sox to their first pennant in twenty-one years. "I don't think I ever saw a pitcher shake off one of his signs. They had too much respect for him," said Boston teammate Tony Conigliaro many years later. Some pitchers and catchers become so in tune with each other that signs are superfluous. In the 1991 *Boston Globe* obituary for catcher Sammy White, who had played for the Red Sox in the 1950s, pitcher Frank Sullivan recollected that when he pitched, White did not use hand signals after the first three innings of the game. "He knew what was coming," Sullivan told the *Globe*. "He just knew. It played heck with the opposition because they couldn't steal any signs and I could quick pitch them."[6]

"There are as many pitching signs as there are fingers on a catcher's hand, areas of his body and gestures of his arm," Jim Brosnan wrote in his 1962 classic, *Pennant Race*. "It is conceivable that a million different combinations of signs could be used during a season."[7]

"Signals are very important but they must be simple," the great catcher and manager George "Birdie" Tebbetts once wrote. "They are of no value if they are so difficult they tend to take the pitcher's mind off the situation. They can be given with the hand, fingers, glove, feet, from the count on the scoreboard, or by the pitcher, but most commonly are flashed as finger signs inside the catcher's thigh."[8]

Without a man on second, a catcher's signals are most likely to be as follows:

1 finger = fastball

2 fingers = curveball

3 fingers = changeup or other breaking ball

Location is often signaled by pointing in the direction where the pitch is to be thrown or by the location where the catcher sets up. Added to these might be a few special situation signs—a closed fist for a pitchout or a thumb jerked up to "knock him down."

All signs change when a runner is on second and in a position to see the catcher's fingers, so his final signs are hidden in a series of finger flashings and "pumps." At its most basic an agreed-upon signal (say, the third one flashed) may be the real one, or it may follow an "indicator" (perhaps the sign after three fingers is first signaled). Catchers also commonly employ a system of "pumps"—combinations of fingers to indicate a pitch after an indicator. For instance, the call for a curveball might follow a few decoy signs (1, 3, 1), an indicator (2), and three pumps (1, 1, 1). The next call, for a fastball, might be an indicator (2) followed by three different pumps (3, 2, 1).

Given all the deception, inevitably signs are missed or misread. A majority of passed balls are the result of such miscues. A catcher having given a sign for a curve sets up low, but the pitcher thought he had called for a fastball and comes in hard and high.

Missed signals are not only the province of the battery. A batter may think he has been told to swing away but instead has been asked to bunt, thereby exposing a base runner, or a shortstop may have been told to cover second but understood that the second baseman would cover, leaving the bag unattended. Such miscues can cost a team a game. Chuck Dressen, who managed in the Majors for sixteen seasons, once said that most losing teams drop enough close games because of missed signals to keep them from being winners. Dressen maintained that baseball writers seldom pick up on the missed-signal story when explaining a defeat.[9]

Sometimes, however, missed signs are so obvious that they cannot be overlooked, even in seemingly ordinary circumstances. In a 2–1 interleague loss to the Dodgers in 2001, with the Mariners' Mark McLemore at first and John Olerud at the plate, a hit-and-run was called for. McLemore ran, but Olerud missed the sign and took the pitch, and McLemore was caught in a rundown. Olerud homered on the next pitch for the Mariners' only run in the 2–1 defeat.

Baseball is a game of deception in many ways. Players refer to this as "gaining the edge" or simply "the edge." Some methods are illegal. Batters such as Albert Belle, Howard Johnson, Norm Cash, and Graig Nettles doctored their bats to give them added spring. Pitchers have lubricated and defaced balls to gain a deceptive edge from the mound. Gaylord Perry and other masters of the art turned their well-earned reputations as spitballers into an imagined threat: by going through suspicious-looking hand-to-mouth-to-cap moves on the mound, batters often lost their concentration, looking for something that may or may not have been there. Many years after the fact, Yankee pitching ace Whitey Ford admitted that catcher Elston Howard helped him on occasion by scuffing the ball against the sharpened edge of his shin guard so it would behave erratically. Some teams groom their fields to hinder opponents or help themselves, and Eddie Stanky, manager of the light-hitting White Sox in the 1960s, was accused of storing baseballs in a freezer to deaden them and shorten the distance they would travel.

Stealing signs and looking for tip-offs, however, are part of the established fabric of the game and are considered ethical, while corked bats and spitballs are not. Tip-offs are what players call the unconscious signs given by pitchers, catchers, base runners, and others on the field. "A lot of guys give away their stuff, and they don't even know they're doing it," then Tigers manager Larry Parrish observed. "It's usually something insignificant, the way they bring their hands together before a pitch, the way they might cock their head for different pitch—or even something as obvious as sticking their finger out of their glove or keeping it in."[10]

Infielder Mike Bordick told the author in a 2001 interview that he studied the pitchers looking for a tip-off to the next pitch. "The indication could be how they hold their glove. Sometimes when the glove is over the pitcher's head it is tipped in different directions, and maybe they tip their glove a certain way on a breaking ball. Or it could be what they are doing with their feet—maybe they are digging in on the mound to get a better grip on a forkball or curveball."

Because the opposition is ever vigilant, managers and coaches keep a close eye on their players' tendencies so as to prevent tip-offs. When Babe Ruth was a young pitcher for the Boston Red Sox, his manager, Bill Carrigan, discovered that Ruth was telegraphing every curveball by curling his tongue in the corner of his mouth. In his youth the ever-loquacious Yogi Berra always chatted with infielders when he got on base. However, whenever he got a hit-and-run sign, he became silent, a tip-off that was not missed by the opposition, which picked him off with some regularity. Eventually, the Yankees taught Berra to keep talking in all situations.[11]

One of baseball's oldest and most enduring axioms is "If you're not stealing, you're not trying." For a coach or manager, the ability to steal signs is as valuable an asset to a team as a player's ability to steal bases. There are men whose careers in the game have been extended by a decade or longer because of their ability to decode the opposition, or, as Tristram Potter Coffin put it in *The Old Ball Game*, "A good sign stealer can always get a job." Art Fletcher, a coach and sign-stealing specialist for the New York Yankees from 1926 to 1945, was believed to have been the highest-paid coach in all of baseball during those twenty seasons. Tommy Henrich credited Fletcher with alerting him for a fastball before he hit one of the longest home runs of his career—one that a writer said was "last seen somewhere over Yonkers."[12]

Successful signs, and sign-stealing, have won countless games over the decades. Any game won with a hit-and-run, bunt, or steal depended on the play being ordered and executed covertly. Conversely, every year a comparable number of games have been lost because a club has not protected its signs or revealed them unconsciously. "Of all the skills wrapped up in the complex game of big league baseball, none is practiced with more ingenuity and less publicity than the fine art of diamond larceny," baseball writer Martin Abramson wrote in the *American Weekly* in 1955. "From the days of the old Orioles to Durocher's Giants, sign-stealers have been surreptitiously deciding crucial ball games and winning world championships."[13]

Though difficult to prove because those involved would hardly admit it, ample evidence exists to suggest that the outcomes of no fewer than three World Series (1913, 1920, and 2001) were affected by the unconscious tipping of pitches to the eventual winner (respectively, Connie Mack's Philadelphia Athletics, the Cleveland Indians, and the Arizona Diamondbacks), involving some of the most famous pitchers in the game, and most recently tippers with names such as Andy Pettitte, Randy Johnson, and Curt Schilling. Assuming that these three Series (and maybe more) were "given away" by what Freud would term the "psychopathology of everyday life" and what a poker player calls "tells," then baseball's sacred statistics deserve some invisible asterisks. A pitcher who was shelled because his catcher gave away his pitches may not deserve his high earned run average (ERA). In a very real sense, responsibility for tipping pitches or plays rests with the team, especially its coaching staff, so it amounts to a team error. Assuming that many games and even the occasional championship were affected by breaking the other teams' codes or using devices outside the lines to steal them, the effect on the game has been spectacular.

Paul Molitor, considered one of the best modern sign stealers, believes the art of sign-stealing is a "part of the game." "If you are able to steal a bunt sign, a hit,-and-run sign, get an out and win an inning, you can win a game that you otherwise might have lost." Molitor makes no bones about the fact that his abilities, coupled with those of his Milwaukee Brewers teammates—most notably Robin Yount—were responsible for several Brewers wins a season when he played for them in the 1980s.

Hall of Famer Ralph Kiner agreed with Molitor when he was interviewed in 2001: "The fault is not with the people stealing the signs, but with the people giving them." Former pitcher and current pitching coach Orel Hershiser, who is by all accounts a man of high moral standards, says, "It is a pitcher's own fault if his signs are picked up; he needs to be smart on the mound and realize that if his signs aren't complicated enough, someone will try to figure them out. Don't be naive and think the opponent wouldn't play that way. Winning and losing is a cutthroat business, and stealing signs is a fair part of the gamesmanship that goes along with playing in the big leagues. It's not cheating."

One of the greatest sign stealers of all times, Del Baker, stated, "There was no such thing as sign stealing, just giveaways," and the upright Hall of Famer Christy Mathewson observed, "No tricks are tolerated in tennis, yet the baseball manager who can devise some scheme by which he disconcerts his opponents is considered a great leader." Others have suggested that "steal" is not the proper word; rather, it should be "interpret."[14]

Yet even sign-stealing is subject to baseball's unwritten code of behavior, and there are, in fact, forms of stealing that baseball today considers dishonorable. That long-established code says that the use of mechanical or electronic devices or the use of anyone not in uniform or outside the confines of the ballpark constitutes cheating. The code dictates that a pitcher in the bullpen can watch the opposing catcher give signals but simply cannot use binoculars or a television monitor to help him and that a runner on second who picks up a signal from the catcher is essentially doing his job. The greatest taboo in today's game is to steal from a point outside the confines of the playing field and dugout. "That's cheating," said Don Zimmer when he was the dugout coach for the New York Yankees. "If you're getting signs from a scoreboard, bullpen, using glasses, to me that's cheatin.'"

The question of the ethics of sign-stealing was resurrected by a *Wall Street Journal* story in early 2000 that revisited charges—which first surfaced in 1962—that sign-stealing, by means of a center-field clubhouse telescope, aided the 1951 New York Giants in their improbable comeback in the weeks leading up to Bobby Thomson's famous pennant-winning home run that has gone down in baseball lore as "The Miracle of Coogan's Bluff." It was critical to the Giants overcoming a thirteen-and-a-half-game deficit that got them in a position to win baseball's most famous pennant race.

A significant part of the history of baseball revolves around the often ingenious attempts to decipher the opposition's signs and mannerisms.

1

From Signal Flags and Torches on the Battlefield to the Early Game

Baseball historian Harold Seymour observed that "to ascertain who invented baseball would be the equivalent of trying to locate the discoverer of fire." The same is true of signs. It is all but impossible to determine the first time a person playing baseball—or baste ball, town ball, rounders, or any of its predecessors—began suggesting plays or pitches to teammates with nonverbal signs.

Such signals and deceptive signs have a long and diverse history in war, especially at sea, where signal flags have for centuries been used by warships to communicate with each other. During the Revolutionary War Yankee privateers sank or captured sixteen of King George's warships and more than twenty-eight hundred merchant ships. The Americans carried collections of foreign flags and used them when traveling in pairs or groups to trick the British: if the enemy was sighted and the commander wanted to order "begin chase," he would raise a British flag at his stern and hoist a pennant; to engage the enemy, the British flag was brought down and replaced with one of any European nation. Simple lantern signals were also used on occasion during the war, including the famous "One if by land, two if by sea" warning from the Old North Church by Paul Revere. In 1855 the British Board of Trade developed the first International Code for peacetime use. It employed eighteen flags to convey seventy thousand visual signals. The code was adopted by most seafaring nations.[1]

Coded communications expanded into many areas during the nineteenth century. In 1817 Thomas Gallaudet, a young Congregational minister from Hartford, Connecticut, opened the first free school for the deaf and brought Laurent Clerc, a deaf sign-language teacher from Paris, to America to develop an American signing system. Other sign languages developed, out of necessity, including the code of workers unable to be heard over the din of the factory floor.[2]

In 1843 Samuel F. B. Morse and Alfred Vail devised the Morse code, and the following year Morse demonstrated the electric telegraph; by 1851 there were 51 telegraph companies in operation.[3] Both coasts were connected by wire in 1861, and there were then 2,250 telegraph offices in operation nationwide. With this came a need for security, as elaborate codes were established for private cable-message traffic so that one's commercial rivals could not gain access to important information.[4]

Indeed, the telegraph was instrumental in both the growth of the American newspaper and the development of baseball as a national sport. It allowed for the instant transmission of scores, standings, and box scores, which could be published in the next morning's edition. In fact, the first known reference to a catcher using signals to move his team into defensive position used the metaphor of the telegraph.[5]

A July 9, 1860, account of a game between the New York Excelsiors and Rochester's Flour City team observed:

> The Excelsiors are poised in every point of the game, and their superb fielding called forth loud cheers from the spectators. Creighton, their pitcher, we think, handles the ball a little the nicest of any man we ever saw. The catcher was also proficient in his part, and won encomiums for the manner in which he would telegraph advantages to

be gained, or the direction as to which one of the fielders should take a "fly." There was no rushing for a ball, but each man of the Excelsiors knew his place and kept it, a point which our ball-players will please make a note of.[6]

Baseball games played by soldiers during the Civil War were an opportunity for the expanded use of signs. "Undoubtedly, the informal signals devised for the battlefield helped expand the system of baseball signs," says David L. Woods, an authority on military communications. "In point of fact, baseball was a very popular recreational pastime during the American Civil War, which was also a war with much use of military signals, both informal and longer range. Although formal evidence is lacking, it seems obvious that many of the men playing baseball during free time in that war may have at the same time devised signs that were similar to the more elementary battlefield signals these same men used for self protection while fighting. There has never been any shortage of ingenuity in either American baseball players nor American fighting men."[7]

The inventor of the system of signals used by the Union and the Confederacy during the Civil War was Albert James Myer, a young army doctor whose medical school thesis was titled "A New Sign Language for Deaf Mutes." Many Confederates had been trained by Myer before the war began. Myer freely admitted his indebtedness to the ancient Greek Polybius, who had invented a system of signals using torches, and to the pantomimic signs of the American Indian with which he had become familiar during excursions into Indian Territory from his prewar post in Texas. In 1860 he applied for a patent on his "Improved System of Signalizing," which was granted on January 29, 1861.[8]

Myer first called his system "flag telegraphy," which he then changed to "torch telegraphy," but it was quickly dubbed "wig-wag" by a Union general. Wig-wag was based on the waving of flags and torches to transmit ciphered signals. His "system" was light enough for a soldier to carry in his backpack and in his head—a white flag with a red square in the center for use against a dark background, a red flag with a white square to be used against light backgrounds, and torches for night use. Telescopes were used to read the signals at distances up to twenty miles.[9]

Myer's former assistant Lieutenant E. P. Alexander became a major force for the Confederates, and during the Battle of Bull Run he spotted a Union movement and sent a signal—"Look to your left, your position is changed"—which turned the tide of battle and gained Alexander a large promotion, enabling him to direct widespread signaling activity throughout the Confederacy. Signaling by torch, flag, and hand was essential to the South because it lacked telegraphic equipment. But the Confederacy was adept at breaking the Northern code, and on several occasions Myer was forced to change his cipher. The Confederates, on the other hand, changed their ciphers daily and were able to move ciphered signals under the noses of their enemy: a secret wig-wag station was also maintained nearly four years within a block or two of the War Department in Washington, sending hourly reports to a post across the Potomac in Confederate territory."[10]

Despite signals' proven utility and tactical importance, there were some who simply did not trust them during the war. On January 26, 1863, Joseph Hooker, who took over the Army of the Potomac on January 23, 1863, from Ambrose Burnside, dismissed his signal officer, Captain Samuel T. Cushing, and sent him to West Point to establish a signal department there. "The officers charged with the discipline of the Academy said that I had 'ruined the service,' since, by several methods not known to the officers, all the cadets could, by winking their eyes, wiping their lips, tapping on gas pipes, etc., etc., communicate information as to inspections going on, and give intelligence in section rooms as to abstruse questions, etc. etc. and consequently the cadets could engage in all sorts of rascality with far less fear of detection than ever before. I thought it quite a compliment of the usefulness of the code." Cushing was promptly transferred away from West Point, leaving in his wake an unintended system of covert and insubordinate signals. By contrast, Hooker's failure to use signals was largely responsible for his defeat at Chancellorsville.[11]

Baseball was popular during the conflict, and the gospel of the game spread, carried to parts of the country where it had not been before. Many rural Southerners first saw the game played by Northern prisoners, and others, like Albert G. Spalding of Rockford, Illinois, learned the game from returning soldiers. There is much personal testimony to the importance of the game in combat zones. George Putnam, a Union soldier stationed in Texas, remembered a particular game. "Suddenly," he recalled, "there came a scattering fire of which the three outfielders caught the brunt; the center field was hit and was captured, the left and right field managed to get back into our lines. The attack . . . was repelled without serious difficulty, but we had lost not only our center field, but . . . the only baseball in Alexandria, Texas."

One of the best-attended sporting events of the nineteenth century took place on Christmas Day, 1862, when the 165th New York Volunteer Regiment played at Hilton Head, South Carolina, against a team selected from other Union regiments, with nearly forty thousand troops watching. A. G. Mills, who would later become the president of the National League and author the game's "basic agreement," played in that game.

Guides and manuals on playing the game proliferated after the Civil War. *Haney's Base Ball Book of Reference* for 1867 suggested, "Always have an understanding with your two sets of fielders in regard to private signals, so as to be able to call them in closer, or place them out further, or nearer the foul-ball lines, as occasion may require, without giving notice to your adversaries."[12]

British-born Harry Wright's 1869 Cincinnati Red Stockings, the first fully compensated professional baseball team, was also the first formal team of any kind to leave evidence that they used coded signs and signals to win baseball games. Ex-cricketer Wright ran his team "like a nicely adjusted machine." The earliest known newspaper account of his innovation—and the first use of the term "signs" in the context of baseball— came when the team swung west in late September to play teams in California. A reporter for the *Daily Alta California* wrote on September 26, 1869, "It must be remembered that the first nine of the Red Stockings are picked men from among the best players of the United States, are in constant practice, and have perfected a stream of telegraphic signals as easily recognized as if spoken words were used. The Red Stockings have really two captains—the ostensible one in the position of 'centre field,' [who] directs movements of the fielders, and the other is the catcher, who indicates by signs to the pitcher and base-keepers the proper thing to do at the right moment." The next day's edition of the *Alta* contained this piece of commentary:

> The Red Stockings have arranged a set of orders so brief that frequently only the name of the player is called and he hastens to do what is requisite: an instance of their alacrity and perfect understanding was given on Saturday—a sky ball was sent between short-stop and right field, for which either might have gone, but the captain called "McVey," and right field at once put himself in position to catch it, but the captain also called "Wright" in the same breath, and short-stop ran and dropped on his knee under McVey's hands, so that if missed by the first it could still be caught before reaching the ground.[13]

Thus, early in baseball's history the catcher's central role as the one who calls the game was established, and it has remained so to the present. The catcher is far better qualified to orchestrate the defensive effort, including the moving of fielders, than anyone else on the team, including the pitcher. He can see all that is happening on the playing field, can observe the batter at close quarters, and gets to see the batters and observe their peculiarities on a much more regular basis. The use of the military term "battery" to describe the pitcher and catcher as a unit was also introduced, with the pitcher playing the role of the man who aims and fires the cannon and the catcher the man who calls the shot.[14]

Sign-stealing early on became an established part of the game. Although it will probably never be known when the first attempts were made to steal signs, baseball writer Dan Daniel traced the first allegations of sign-stealing back to 1876, the year the National League was founded, when that league's Hartford Dark Blues were publicly accused of taking their opponents' signals. "There was a little shack outside the park, hung off a telegraph pole. A lot of dope came out of that little 'office.'"[15] Though it would be years before this would be known as sign-stealing—the players called it "tipping off the signs," clearly implying that it was the opposition guilelessly giving away the signs to those accepting the tips—the tactic had great natural appeal as both a challenge and an opportunity.

Signs and the lore surrounding them became part of the culture of baseball as the game progressed in its early years. Larry Corcoran of the Chicago White Stockings is widely credited as the first big-league pitcher to work out a system of signals with his catcher. Corcoran's system involved his catcher moving a wad of tobacco to different sides of his mouth. Clearly, the system worked, as Corcoran won forty-three games in his rookie season of 1880. Another account credits Silver Flint with the tobacco signal, while another suggests that Chicago's catcher-outfielder Mike "King" Kelly invented the modern system of finger signals by which one finger was a call for a fastball and two for a curve.

Beginning in the late 1870s, as "management" became a larger part of the game, coaches began patrolling the first and third base lines, their roles based on military convention. The manager was the general, and his coaches were lieutenants, conveying his instructions to the players to keep the offensive attack moving. A new kind of signaling then emerged, called wig-wagging after Myer's Civil War signal system, which allowed the coaches to pass along coded instructions to the batter and base runners.

In 1887 coaches were formally recognized in the official rules, and coach's boxes were established fifteen feet from the base-lines to contain Cap Anson and other noisy distracters who ran up and down the baselines baiting and belittling the opposition. The first and third base coaches began to systematically steal from the opposition and pass information along to the batter. In his 1888 primer, *Base-Ball—How to Become a Player*, John Montgomery Ward, shortstop of the New York Giants, explained how coaches were in a fine position to steal signs from a catcher and then "make some remark with no apparent reference to the batter, but really previously agreed upon, to notify him of what kind of ball is going to be pitched. This known, the batter has nothing to do but pick out his ball and lay on it with all his weight." Ward said that the Giants had "great sport" stealing and transmitting signals in this manner during a winter tour of California.[16]

A dramatic example of the value of a coach's signs involved left-handed batter William Ellsworth Hoy, an extremely talented deaf player who carried the unfortunate nickname of Dummy—although writers of the time were always quick to point out that he possessed far more than the average degree of brightness. Hoy was the second deaf player in the professional game and one of the leading players at the turn of the century.[17]

In his rookie season of 1888, playing for the Washington National League team, Hoy was having trouble keeping track of the count, as he had to turn around and try to read the umpire's lips. He and his managers and coaches worked out an overt system, which he carried from team to team: if the third base coach pointed his index fingers to the right, the ump had called a strike, and if he pointed the left, it was a ball. The season before this system was established, Hoy was confused and susceptible to "quick" pitches coming before he knew the count. It was all a matter of timing for a man whose major asset was speed.[18]

Hoy stole 594 bases in his career, underscoring the point that he was adroit at nonverbal communications. A popular and exciting outfielder, who in one 1889 game threw three players out at home, he inspired fans to signal their silent approval. "When fielder Hoy made a brilliant catch, the crowd arose en masse, and wildly waved hats and arms. It was the only way in which they could testify their appreciation to the deaf mute athlete," wrote Henry Fumess in an 1892 issue of *Sporting Life*.[19]

The brainier players soon found other signals that could spell the difference between winning and losing. In 1888 Connie Mack, a catcher for the Washington National League team, and a pitcher named "Grasshopper" Jim Whitney developed a system of signals to prevent base stealing at a time when it was rampant. "In those days base runners just ran; the pitcher never did anything to stop them," Mack told H. G. Salsinger of the *Detroit News* shortly before his death. "Grasshopper and I decided we'd change things. I told him that I would watch the base runner and when I saw one of them taking an extra-long lead I would move my right foot. Grasshopper would then go through with his full windup but, instead of pitching to the batter, he would whirl and throw to the man covering the base."

Mack said that it severely cut down on base stealing, although two players, John Montgomery Ward of the Giants and King Kelly of Chicago, caught on to what they were doing. "They were a couple of smart lads and they kept their discovery to themselves," said Mack.[20]

"Scientific baseball" had arrived, and increasingly books and articles appeared that referred to the game as one of brain work and mathematical precision. In 1889 N. Fred Pfeffer, the bare-handed infield star and tactician with the Chicago White Stockings of the 1880s (who, for reasons obscured by time, carried the nickname "Dandelion"), published a manual called *Scientific Ball*. It described the tenets of scientific play for, as he put it in the introduction, "those millions interested."

Pfeffer's science was based on common sense and the best conventional wisdom of the time. At the heart of his defensive science was a "code of motions so perfected" that every man on a club knew what kind of a ball was to be pitched next. "Knowing this in advance, the men can so place themselves as to give the man in the box [the pitcher] the most effective support." Pfeffer's words echo the principles of defensive baseball as they are practiced today:

> When a right-handed pitcher delivers a low curve to a left-handed batter, the probabilities are that the hit will be to right field. If the first and second basemen know that such a ball is to be pitched, it gives them a special warning to be on the alert. If the ball delivered to a left-handed batter is to be a high one, the first and second basemen, upon getting the sign, should move up toward second, as you cannot pull a high ball around as you can a low one. A low, curve ball delivered by a right-handed pitcher to a right-handed batter will naturally go to left field. A fast, straight ball is more liable to go to right field. The best

pitcher I know of locates his fielders and then pitches accordingly, so as to compel the batter as far as possible to hit in the desired direction.[21]

Pfeffer believed that the fielder's job was to move at the very last moment when the pitcher was in his delivery and that once a play had begun, it was imperative that the players knew how to back one another up. "Failure to 'back up' players and positions has probably been as disastrous a feature of losing-clubs as any other which can be specified," he wrote. "Because of this fatal weakness scores of otherwise well-played games are needlessly sacrificed each year."[22]

New offensive plays were developed in response to defensive schemes and the ability to secretly signal and coordinate one's teammates, and the hit-and-run play is a good example. By prearrangement with the batter a base runner starts to run to the next base as soon as the pitcher delivers the ball to the batter, who must try to hit it behind the runner to protect him. The play is usually undertaken with a runner on first base only: as he heads to second base, either the shortstop or the second baseman moves to cover the bag, giving the batter a gap in the infield defense through which to direct the ball. If the batter gets a hit, the base runner is usually able to advance to third base. If the ball is hit to an infielder, the base runner's head start reduces the defense's chance of turning the double play. However, if the batter swings and misses, the runner may be thrown out, and if the ball is hit for a pop fly or a line drive, the runner is likely to become the second out.

Several individuals have been credited with "inventing" the hit-and-run, including Ned Hanlon, John McGraw, and "Wee Willie" Keeler. However, it may have resulted from a missed signal and been introduced accidentally by a player on the Louisville American Association team in the 1880s. "Pete Browning was the originator of the hit-and-run game," Philadelphia Athletics third baseman Lave Cross wrote.

He was hard of hearing, and one day he couldn't hear the coacher after getting to first on a hit, and started for second on the first ball pitched. He ran like a wildcat and got to third on a single. Pete would not have gotten past second had he not misunderstood the signals, or if he could have heard the coacher. As it was, when he started off on his mad run he got to third safely, and would have been on the way home if he hadn't been held by the man coaching on third. Hughey [sic] Jennings heard of it, and the system was introduced in Baltimore and worked with great success."[23]

Others besides Baltimore perfected the hit-and-run and other acts of teamwork based on signals between players. "I have never, in my twelve years experience on the diamond, seen such skillful playing." wrote John Montgomery Ward, then manager of the rival New York Giants, about Frank Selee's 1893 Boston National League club, the Beaneaters. "The Boston players use more head-work and private signals than any other team in the country, and that alone is the reason why they can win the championship with such apparent ease." The epitome of their brand of baseball was the hit-and-run play. "Man may penetrate the outer reaches of the universe, he may solve the very secret of eternity itself but for me, the ultimate human experience is to witness the flawless execution of the hit-and-run," Branch Rickey said many years later.[24]

The art of running an offense on well-rehearsed, coordinated signals was also refined by the Beaneaters' National League rival, the Baltimore Orioles of the late 1890s, managed by Ned Hanlon. He used coded signals to order "plays"—sacrifice bunts, double steals, squeezes, hit-and-runs—that were, by all accounts, perfected by John McGraw and Willie Keeler. During spring training in New Orleans in 1894, with the enthusiastic encouragement of Hanlon, McGraw began to devise plays calculated to upset the opposition, and they all polished their bunting game. As Frank Graham said in his 1944 biography of McGraw, "They invented so many tricks that, in order to curb them, the owners of the other clubs had to draft new rules or change some of the old ones."[25]

Jack Glasscock, a bare-handed shortstop who played for eight teams between 1879 and 1895, is credited with being the first infielder to signal the catcher as to whether the shortstop or second baseman would cover second base in the event that a runner on first tried to steal. Shortstop Monte Cross, active in the Major Leagues from 1892 through 1907, was one of the first to signal his outfielders regarding the location of the next pitch so they could anticipate where it might be hit. He perfected his system while playing for Connie Mack's Athletics, and at the end of his career *The Sporting News* claimed that Cross was "the greatest ever for signs."

By the spring of 1915, *The Sporting News* observed that most teams were using infielders to relay signals from the catcher to the outfield. Citing the examples of Cross and Johnny Evers, "two men known as base ball's best for brains in their own period," the newspaper asserted that not letting the outfield in on the next pitch had unconsciously "lost many ball games."

As signals proliferated, codes of on-field behavior developed out of them and were well established by the turn of the century. A player who disregarded a bunt sign or ran through a coach's stop sign was reprimanded or fined, or both, even though his disregard had yielded him a hit or an extra base. While pitchers were not required to accept their catchers' calls, they were obliged to signal for a different pitch by shaking their heads so catchers were not crossed up and could alert the rest of the team as to what kind of pitch was going to be thrown.

2

The Devious Devices of the
Buzzer and Binocular Era

On September 17, 1900, in the third inning of the first game of a doubleheader between the Reds and the Phillies at Philadelphia's Baker Bowl, the 4,771 fans in attendance were treated to one of organized baseball's most outrageous moments, a scene unequaled before or since. Cincinnati shortstop and team captain Tommy Corcoran, concerned that his pitcher, Ted Breitenstein, was being shelled, was drawn to the odd way in which the Phillies' third base coach, Pearce "Petie" Chiles, was planting his foot in exactly the same spot before each pitch.

Suddenly, Corcoran let out a loud yell, ran across the third base line, and began frantically kicking the ground around the third base coaching area, using his spikes and hands to remove large clods of dirt. Fans thought he had gone mad. Within moments the groundskeeper, umpire Tim Hurst, both teams, and several police officers surrounded Corcoran, who eventually unearthed a small wooden box containing an electric buzzer with wires attached.

Cincinnati and the other teams in the league had become suspicious that the Phillies were stealing signs at their home park. Joe Dittmar, in his definitive investigation into this incident, notes, "The Phillies had the best home record (45-23) in the league, yet on the road they ranked fourth with a losing ledger (30-40). Guests had suspected foul play since the prior season but could never quite satisfy their suspicions until the day . . . when the Phillies were caught with their hands and feet in the cookie jar."[1]

In the following days a picture emerged of a scheme run by two men. Morgan Murphy, a second-string, light-hitting catcher with the Phillies who had sat out the 1899 season, was assigned to the club's center-field clubhouse. He sat by a peephole where he used binoculars to steal signs from the opposing catcher. Murphy employed a Morse-code key rigged to an underground telegraphic system to signal Coach Chiles as to the upcoming pitch—one dash for a fastball, two for curve, and three for a slow ball or change of pace. Chiles stood with his foot above the device and felt the signals as "vibrathrobs."[2]

Confronted with the evidence, the Phillies' brass denied everything. Murphy was quickly dubbed "the Thomas Edison of baseball" by press wags, and Chiles was similarly ridiculed. Before Cincinnati left town Chiles staged a mild act of revenge by pretending to be receiving signals through his feet. This time when the Reds charged the spot and dug it up, they found a plain board with no wires or buzzer that Chiles had planted early that morning.

Philadelphia headed to Brooklyn, where, on September 26, Murphy was accused of stealing signs from the window of a tenement with a pair of binoculars and flashing signals to Chiles with a folded newspaper. On the twenty-ninth Cincinnati visited Pittsburgh, where Tommy Corcoran went into action again. This time he zeroed in on a tiny fenced-off area in deep center field into which he a boosted teammate—145-pound "Little Phil" Geier—who discovered field glasses and a long L-shaped rod. The Pittsburgh system involved the letter O on the fence into which the L-shaped iron was placed. Signs were relayed directly to the batter as the iron bar was moved like the hand of a clock: if it pointed to noon, it was a fastball; three o'clock, an inside curve; and nine o'clock, an outside curve.

As it turned out, the Phillies and the Pirates had known of each other's systems and agreed that neither would spy on the other. When, for example, the Pirates were in Philadelphia, Morgan Murphy sat on the bench with the rest of the players as a show of "good faith." The nonaggression pact had been established early in 1900 when a player was traded to the Pirates from the Phillies.

This realization set off a storm of protest, accusation, and proposed punishment. The Brooklyn Superbas, then the official nickname of the team many were calling the Dodgers, called for having the Phillies' batting averages and final standings forever expunged from the record books. Others urged for a new rule that would make the umpire take a roll call of both teams before the game began to make sure that a coach or nonstarting player was not out working a sign-stealing system.

Pressure was put on the Phillies for an explanation, which finally came on October 2 in a statement from Colonel John I. Rogers, Phillies director and treasurer, who denied any use of the electrical device, insisting that it was part of a lighting system that had been left there by a carnival company that had occupied the field for a few days in July. "It is absolutely too silly to further discuss the subject, and I therefore dismiss it. I will certainly not dignify the charge by pleading 'not guilty,'" Rogers stated in an attempt to close the matter.

But it would not close. Less than a week after the Rogers press conference, reporter Charles Dryden of the *New York North American* revealed the whole story. Chiles originally proposed the idea of using field glasses to steal signs and pass them along using a rolled-up newspaper—holding the paper horizontally signified a curveball and vertically a fastball. This soon became too obvious, and Chiles, who had once stepped on a live wire, came up with the buzzer scheme.[3]

Rather than deter others, the "vibrathrob" episode seemed to encourage them. The next season the Phillies' crosstown rivals, the Athletics, were implicated when a club employee, also named Murphy, stationed himself on the roof of a building across from the stadium and picked up signs with the help of high-powered binoculars, then indicating the next pitch by manipulating a weather vane.

Amid the proliferation of sign-stealing, umpires began to use signals to announce their decisions publicly, in order to give the fans a better idea of what was going on. Crowds were growing, and it was becoming harder to hear the umpires' bellowed verbal calls.

Like so many other elements of baseball history, it is hard to determine exactly when this practice began. In a letter to the editor published in the March 27, 1870, *New York Sunday Mercury*, Cincinnati Red Stockings manager Harry Wright wrote, "There is one thing I would like to see the umpire do at [a] big game, and that is, raise his hand when a man is out. You know what noise there is always when a fine play is made on the bases, and it being impossible to hear the umpire, it is always some little time before the player knows whether he is given out or not. It would very often save a great deal of bother and confusion."[4]

Some years after Wright's appeal, a deaf umpire used hand signals to communicate with the players on the field. According to baseball historian Bill Deane, Ed Dundon, who had pitched in the Major Leagues in 1883–84, was the innovator. The November 6, 1886, edition of *The Sporting News* reported that "Dundon, the deaf . . . pitcher of the Acid Iron Earths, umpired a game at Mobile between the Acids and Mobiles, on October 20. . . . He used the fingers of his right hand to indicate strikes, the fingers of the left to call balls, a shake of the head decided a man 'not out,' and a wave of the hand meant out."[5]

A 1966 letter in the files of the National Baseball Library in Cooperstown, New York, written by retired brigadier general R. J. Burt, offers additional information on the origins of umpires' signals. His father, Andrew Sheridan Burt, also a brigadier general, was a distinguished veteran of the Civil War and wherever he was posted established baseball teams in the belief that the sport heightened esprit de corps and served to entertain the troops. His teams would play each other and sometimes go on Fourth of July barnstorming tours to play teams in nearby towns. Andrew Burt was soon known as "Mr. Army Base Ball Man."

In 1898, when the Spanish-American War broke out, the elder Burt was joined by his son, an army officer and ardent lover of the game who had played at West Point, at a staging area for the war involving several regiments that had been established at Chickamauga Park, Georgia. The son was soon calling balls and strikes and, according to his letter, quickly learned tricks of the trade from the older umpires on the field. One of these was to pick up a pebble with the right hand after calling a strike and with the left when a ball was called, thus having "an accurate marker to show in case of heated riots, which were many."

His letter then reported on one particular Sunday afternoon when two teams were locked in a fierce rivalry attended by a large and noisy crowd that had moved so close to the action that the catchers had little room to maneuver. "It became necessary, as Umpire," he wrote, "to raise an arm high in the air; right for a strike, left for a ball. Naturally the pebbles were bound to slide out of hand. I was an alert little 'shave tail' then and substituted upright fingers for pebbles. This pleased Mr. Army Base Ball Man greatly."

In the spring of 1902 the elder Burt retired to Washington DC, where he attended an American League (AL) game and was frustrated that he was unable to hear the umpire's ball and strike call. He penned a letter to American League president Ban Johnson, suggesting the use of arm signals. According to his son's 1966 letter, "Mr. Johnson replied cordially and directed his umpires to put this into effect with one modification: The hand signal for strikes was sufficient, since if the fans saw no signal they knew the call was a ball." In return the old general was given an annual pass for American League games until his death in 1915.[6]

Other claims to the invention of umpires' signals can be found. W. A. Phelon Jr. wrote in the September 14, 1901, issue of *Sporting Life*:

Noiseless umpiring is to be attempted at the South Side park [in Chicago] Monday afternoon. Impossible as this may seem at first hearing, it is to be attempted, and there are even bets that it will be a go. George W. Hancock, famed in Chicago as the man who invented indoor base-ball, will be responsible for the success or failure of the scheme. The umpire is to wear a red sleeve on the right arm and a white one on the left. For a strike he will raise the right arm, for a ball the left. . . . People at the far end of the park, unable to hear even that human buffalo, Sheridan, can see the colors, and there seems a good chance for the trick to make a hit.[7]

A popular and oft-repeated story has it that umpiring signals were introduced for the benefit of the aforementioned deaf William Hoy, who played between the years 1888 and 1902. The story has been a very popular one, even to the point of inspiring a 1988 off-Broadway play entitled *The Signal Season of Dummy Hoy*. It is well established that Hoy's coaches and teammates used signals to communicate with him, but there is no evidence that umpire signals were invented on his behalf.[8] The argument has been made by many that Hoy deserves accolades for his accomplishments without the embellishment of the signals story. Sam Crawford, elected to the Baseball Hall of Fame in 1957, told Lawrence Ritter in *The Glory of Their Times* (1984), "Did you know that he once threw three men out at home plate in one game. From the outfield, I mean. That was in 1889. And still they don't give him a tumble for the Hall of Fame. It's not right." The feat of throwing three out from the outfield in one game is still unequaled.

Hoy was on the Chicago White Stockings in 1901 when the colored-sleeve idea was proposed, but there is no suggestion that the sleeves were intended for anyone other than the fans. The 1909 *Spalding Guide* includes an article, "Semaphore Signals by Umpires," which does not mention Hoy, nor does it mention Hall of Fame umpire Bill Klem of the National League, who is officially recognized on his bronze Cooperstown plaque as "introducing arm signals indicating strikes and fair or foul balls." In a 1952 interview with *Collier's* magazine, Klem credited an attorney with suggesting a signal of fair or foul to avoid trouble with fans during a game in 1904. Klem noted better communication helped quell fan and player unrest and made the games more enjoyable and less contentious.

Umpires in both leagues fought the idea of signals, asserting that the waving of their arms distracted from the "dignity" of their calling. The demands of fans and the persistence of league officials finally prevailed, and even the older umpires finally consented. By the 1906–7 seasons umpires had adopted a full system of explanatory signals. Over time, different umpires affected their own signature gestures in the same manner that certain batters created their own distinctive stances. Bill McGowan's 1951 textbook, used in his own school for umpires, offered a variety of options for a called strike, including Red Ormsby's raising his hand high above his head and pointing at the sky, Bill Summers's raising his arm and snapping off a strike in the direction of first base, and McGowan's own closed fist held about four inches above his head.[9]

The signal career of Ty Cobb began in 1905. He stole 892 bases in twenty-four regular seasons—it has been said he played twice as hard and thrice as long as the players of his generation—and loved especially to steal home and to show how good he was in what amounted to one-man shows. On July 22, 1909, for the first of four times in his career, Cobb stole second, third, and home in the seventh inning against the Red Sox. On May 12, 1911, Cobb's Tigers beat the Highlanders, 6–5, as Cobb scored from first on a short single to right field, scored from second on a wild pitch, and stole home with the winning run.

Even though he was very fast on the base paths—once timed running the one-hundred-yard dash in ten seconds—his genius was based on knowing when the pitcher was going to the plate and identifying any signal that the pitcher would throw over to first base. Cobb, who saw the ballpark as a book to be read, looked for mannerisms and tip-offs more than he tried to steal signs. He maintained that his secret against Cy Young, off whom he often stole, was that when the great pitcher was going to throw to first, he would stand on the mound with his arms slightly away from his body, but when his elbows were pulled in it meant he was going to pitch.

Cobb, whose many flaws included a belief in pseudoscience, claimed that his knowledge of phrenology told him that Walter Johnson was an even-tempered gentleman too timid to hit anyone with a ball. Cobb therefore crowded the plate, and Johnson, apparently not willing to harm Cobb, had to pitch him outside, where Cobb could hit the ball to the opposite field. In his sixty-seven career games against Johnson, Cobb hit .355 against the all-time shutout leader. Cobb also felt that Johnson was the easiest pitcher to read. "Since he had all that speed, his catcher always signaled for a fast ball, never anything else," Cobb noted after his playing days were over. "If Johnson shook off the signal, we knew the curve was on its way."

If Cobb was the greatest reader of inadvertent tips, it is ironic that he could be read by others. Buck Crouse, catcher for the White Sox from 1923 to 1930 who was very effective at catching Cobb stealing, said in an interview after his playing days were over, "Cobb was a guy that when he took a big lead, he wouldn't run. When he took a short lead, he was gone. So after I watched him just one time, I knew exactly what he was going to do." In 1948 Arthur Daley of the *New York Times* told of a catcher—"unfortunately I disremember his name," Daley wrote—who habitually pounced on bunts laid down by Cobb. Over time, Cobb became curious about this and in his twenty-third year in the game asked the catcher point-blank why he was so successful. "I suppose it's safe to tell you now, Ty. You're about at the end of your playing days. But I've noticed that just before you're going to bunt, you wet your lower lip with your tongue."

Though Cobb was a master of reading other players' mannerisms, he also benefited from a system that stole from opposing catchers routinely. When Cobb came up in 1905, and in the few years following, the spyglass era was in full swing. "At our Detroit park there was a fellow in center field with a pair of glasses strong enough to bring out the fillings in the catcher's teeth," he admitted in an article for *Life* magazine in 1952 titled "Tricks That Won Me Ball Games." Near him was an advertisement on the fence that read THE DETROIT NEWS: BEST NEWSPAPER IN THE WEST. Cobb wrote, "If you watched the B in that advertisement closely, you would watch little slots open and close. If the slot was open in the top half of the B, our spotter had picked off the signal for a fast ball. If the slot in the bottom of the B opened we knew a curve was coming. I don't know whether the ad sold any newspapers, but it was a great thing for the Detroit batting averages."

On the other hand, Cobb had little interest in his own team's signs. In 1905 at age eighteen, when Cobb joined the Tigers, he was offered the team's signals by his new skipper, Bill Armour, but held up his hand and asked not to use them. "Can't I play my own way?" he asked. "Suit yourself," Armour replied.

Cobb apparently got over this aversion to managerial signs, but because of his toxic personality he had to make special arrangements to get them and to pass along the ones he initiated on his own. "I was one of Ty's best friends when we were with the Tigers and one of his few friends among the players," said Davy Jones to *The Sporting News* shortly after Cobb's death in 1961.

> You could say that Wild Bill Donovan and I were about the only Tigers who were friendly with Cobb when we were winning pennants for Detroit in 1907–09. He was kind of hard to get along with, but he was misunderstood too, and a lot of the abuse he had to take was uncalled for. I led off in those years; Donie Bush batted second, Cobb third and Sam Crawford fourth. Crawford and Bush wouldn't speak to Cobb, or Ty to them. It got so bad that they wouldn't tell each other when they changed signals, which was frequently in those days. So I became a sort of intermediary signal corps. Donie and Sam would let me know what was going on and I would relay the signs to Cobb.[10]

The most notable follower of the Murphy-Chiles school of creative sign-stealing was George Stallings, who in 1897 and 1898 had managed the Phillies, where he had become good friends with Murphy. Stallings was out of baseball for the 1900 season but was well aware of Murphy's ingenious scheme.

In 1909 when he came back to baseball after a long absence as manager of the New York Highlanders—the Yankees as a name was not yet official though already in common use—Stallings realized that the buzzer-box system had its limitations, so he reverted to a wireless solar-powered scheme. He rented an apartment opposite the Hilltop Grounds that provided a clear view of home plate. A spotter armed with a pair of field glasses sat in the apartment window to steal catchers' signs and relay them to Highlander batters with flashes of sunlight bounced off a mirror. The system worked perfectly save for days when the sky was overcast, and on those Stallings moved the operation to a spot behind the outfield fence. From there his operatives manipulated the crossbar in the letter *H* of the word "Hat" in an advertising sign. A black crossbar signified a fastball, while a white bar meant a breaking ball.[11]

Throughout the season speculation about the Highlanders was widespread, and on September 27, 1909, charges of sign-stealing were finally made public in *Sporting Life*. Washington manager Joe Cantillon had been the first to figure out the scheme, which he confirmed by sending his trainer, Jerry Ettinger, out to spy on the spy. Ettinger told *Sporting Life* that the man who did the stealing was "an old-time pitcher" later identified as Gene McCann, who would become a top Yankee scout. Cantillon told Detroit Tiger manager Hughie Jennings, who sent his own trainer out beyond the fence during the Yankees' final home stand of the 1909 season and caught the spy in the act. He then closed down Stallings' operation by sending his men to demolish the scoreboard— one account claimed that it was burned to the ground—and Detroit took three of four from the New Yorkers, the club's only losses in their final seventeen home games. Detroit's own spy system remained undetected until Cobb's 1952 *Life* magazine tell-all.

Detroit won the pennant by beating Connie Mack's Athletics, who claimed that the games the Highlanders stole from them—mainly a key series in which New York took three of four—cost them the pennant. Despite Stallings's determination, the Highlanders finished in fifth place.

Although the Highlanders' antics were greeted with horror by league officials, the New York press dismissed the charges as sour grapes. Writer Joe Vila in *The Sporting News* admitted to the discovery of "a couple of holes in the boards," adding that such transgressions were commonplace and violated no rule that he knew of. Despite this attitude, an ethical line was drawn between stealing with the naked eye inside the confines of the park and using mechanical devices to steal from a point beyond the fences.

The 1910 season brought renewed charges against Stallings and the Highlanders, this time leveled by Ed Walsh, Chicago's star spitballer, and by Joe Cantillon, still managing the hapless Washington team. "I will pay five hundred dollars to any person who produces proof that any improper means to detect signals are used by an American League club," said American League president Ban Johnson, getting no takers.

An odd claim was made by Ed "the Old Fan" Goewey, who strongly suggested in his column for *Leslie's Illustrated* that there was nothing to the 1910 charges. "Recently, new charges of 'signal tipping' have caused some excitement in the baseball world, but, as in the past, have proven to be nothing more than an effort by weaklings to cover up their own shortcomings by alleging misperformance on the part of others."[12]

Goewey spent most of his column lambasting the accusers, calling Washington, among other things, "a team that was once a factor in baseball but which is now a sort of Humpty Dumpty in the national sport" and "a team that for a long time past has done little but spill its baseball milk over its baseball bib."[13] Goewey seemed to be implying that the greater sin was complaining, and baseball's hierarchy appeared to agree with his position, despite the obvious proof.

Stallings was out of baseball for two years, reemerging to manage the Braves to fifth place in 1913. Then, during the "miracle" season of 1914, with his team firmly in possession of eighth place in mid-July, the Braves suddenly caught fire, winning thirty-four of their final forty-four games to surge past the New York Giants and capture the 1914 National League pennant by an astounding ten and a half games. Nobody ever accused Stallings of being up to his old tricks, although more than a few people over time have wondered about this miraculous comeback.

The first decade of the century proved that the best teams had the greatest ability to play the scientific game. C. H. Claudy, one of the leading baseball writers of the time, wrote of the Chicago Cubs, who won the World Series in 1907 and 1908 and the National League pennant in 1910, that they were able to beat "other clubs as good or better than they were because of the perfection of their 'inside base-ball' engineered entirely by signs."

A case in point came at the end of a head-to-head contest between Frank Chance's Cubs and John McGraw's Giants. Well known for their famous infield, immortalized in Franklin P. Adams's poem "Baseball's Sad Lexicon," also known as "Tinker to Evers to Chance," the 1908 Cubs were deadlocked with the New York Giants for first place as the season roared to an exciting end.[14]

What happened in that September 23 Cubs-Giants game is well known to baseball aficionados: Rookie Giant first baseman Fred Merkle failed to touch second base when Al Bridwell delivered an apparent game-winning hit in the bottom of the ninth inning. Merkle headed for the Giant clubhouse in center field, but Evers had noticed that Merkle had not touched second base. By the time the Cubs retrieved the ball and "forced" Merkle at second, fans had swarmed the field, and with order impossible to restore, the game was declared a 1–1 tie. The teams wound up with identical 98-55-1 records, meaning the playoff game would have to be replayed.[15]

After days of official indecision, it was decided that the Polo Grounds would host a second finale on October 8. Nearly a quarter of a million fans showed up to watch the replay. The gates were closed at 1:30 for the 3:00 game because the stadium was filled and tens of thousands were still trying to get in. Firemen with high-pressure hoses knocked down fans who tried to scale the walls, while other fans stormed the gates. A crowd estimated at forty thousand watched from Coogan's Bluff above the Polo Grounds, while others climbed telegraph poles. Two fans were killed when they fell from a pillar on the elevated subway platform. The crowd was rowdy and restless. Giants fans threw bottles at the Cubs, but manager Frank Chance heaved them right back, injuring one spectator.

Toward the end of the game the score was tied, and the Cubs had runners on first and third with Joe Tinker at the plate with the count 1-0. Suddenly, from the Cubs' bench, in the words of Johnny Evers, "there was a movement. A player with earnest, but rather weary face, immobile even in the moment when the whole result of his year's work might be ruined, raised his right hand to his cap, lifted it an inch from his head, replaced it and without a muscle of his face twitching sat watching." This triggered a coach to alert Harry Steinfeldt on first and Frank "Wildfire" Schulte on third.

As the pitcher wound up for his second pitch to Tinker, Steinfeldt ran twenty feet toward second, stopped dead in his tracks, and headed back toward first. Tinker swung and missed, and the catcher relaxed and dropped his arm, preparing to toss the ball back to the pitcher. At that moment Steinfeldt reversed himself again and took off for second at full speed. The Giants catcher hesitated for a split second and then fired the ball to second just as Schulte broke down the line from third. Evers recalled, "An instant later, in a whirling cloud of dust, a runner pivoted around the plate, his foot dragging across the rubber just as the ball, hastily hurled back to the catcher, came down upon his leg. The run had scored. The game was won."

When Tinker had gone to the plate he had been ordered to hit-and-run, but when the first pitch was a ball player-manager Frank Chance had lifted his cap and ordered the delayed double steal. For the first time in the game the coaches called the men on base by their names, which indicated the delayed double steal. Tinker was told to swing and miss. "Chance had won the game from the bench when he lifted his hat from his head."

From this the Cubs went on to win the World Series from the Detroit Tigers, four games to one. The 1908 championship was the last one for the Cubs franchise until 2016.[16]

3

Psychological Warfare

In the early twentieth century baseball became more and more of a head game in which rumor, falsehood, and good acting made it hard to distinguish the real from the imagined, especially when it came to signs and sign-stealing. A hint of larceny published by the right baseball writer, or an ambiguous boast by a player, could cause a team to think its plans were an open secret. Back-to-back World Series underscored the extent that psychological warfare had become part of the game.

When the Philadelphia Athletics defeated the heavily favored Chicago Cubs in the 1910 World Series, it was alleged that Connie Mack's players and coaches had stolen the Cubs' pitching signs and won the championship because they knew what to expect. Hugh Fullerton, the era's premier baseball writer, later reported that the Cubs had held a closed-door meeting on the eve of the Series and been warned that Mack would do everything within his power to get their signs. After losing the first game 4–1 and the second 9–3, they revamped their signals, convinced that they had been stolen and that their fortunes would change. The next day they were blown out 12–5 and a scapegoat was sought, as the Cubs won only one game in the lopsided Series.[1]

Christy Mathewson in his *Pitching in a Pinch* reported, "By a strange kink in the ethics of baseball John Kling, the Chicago catcher, was blamed by the other players on the defeated team for the signs being stolen. They charged that he had been careless in covering his signals and that the enemy's coachers, particularly Topsy Hartsel, a clever man at it, had seen them from the lines. This was really the cause of Kling leaving the Cubs and going to Boston in 1911."[2]

Kling insisted that he was not guilty and had taken every precaution, including changing his signs every three innings. Teammate Johnny Evers, one of baseball's canniest players, sided with Kling, as did Mathewson, who observed, "The Chicago pitchers were away off form in the series and could not control the ball, thus getting themselves 'into the hole' all the time. Shrewd Connie Mack soon realized this and ordered his batters to wait everything out, to make the twirlers throw every ball possible. The result was that, with the pitcher continually in the hole, the batters were guessing what was coming and frequently guessing right, as any smart hitter could under the circumstances. This made it look as if the Athletics were getting the Cubs' 'signals.'"[3]

Fullerton too felt Kling had been wronged and insisted that it was the ineptitude of the pitchers who were tipping their pitches. Writing in *American Magazine*, he based his doubts about sign-stealing on the fact that he watched the game sitting next to Ty Cobb, who called each Cub pitch before it was thrown based on the pitcher's tip-offs and not on any broken code. He surmised that the A's were doing the same thing.

Ever the ethicist, Mathewson was clear on one point: even if the Athletics had stolen the championship, he wrote, "it is no smirch on the character of the club, for they stole honestly." Mathewson loved to tell of an Englishman he once met who told him, "You have such jolly funny morals in this bally country. You steal and rob in baseball and yet you call it fair."[4]

If nothing else, the Series underscored again the power that Mack had as a tactician and a controller of the game via the use of signals—often transmitted by the way in which he handled his scorecard, moved his hat, or placed his hands. "Opposing pitchers have studied [Mack] for years without getting a clue to what his signals mean," Hugh Fullerton wrote of him in the summer of 1911, Mack's fourteenth season as a manager.[5]

In the 1911 World Series Mack's Athletics defeated John McGraw's New York Giants four games to two. Led by Chief Bender, the A's outpitched Christy Mathewson and Rube Marquard, while Frank Baker earned his "Home Run" nickname by homering in Games Two and Three for key wins.

Sign-stealing was widely suspected, and it was alleged, but never proven, that the Athletics' secret agent in stealing signs from Mathewson and Marquard was a hunchbacked mascot and batboy named Louis Van Zelst who dressed in the team uniform and sat on the bench with the team. Baseball writer C. L. Claudy explained, "Many patrons of the game will recall having seen him with a big catcher's mitt, tossing and catching the ball with a pitcher before a game. According to these stories, this bat-boy would see the Giant signals when he walked out to pick up the bat the batsman discarded. Being near the ground, on account of his small stature, he was supposed to be able to see under the catcher's bent knee. Learning the signal, he would transmit it by signs to the coacher on third, who would inform the batsman what variety of pitched ball was coming."[6]

Mathewson never appears to have commented publicly on the story of Van Zelst, but he suspected something was afoot. "When the Giants went to Philadelphia in 1911 for the first game of the world's series in the enemy's camp, I kept watching the windows of the houses just outside of the park for suspicious movements, but could discover none." So fearful was Mathewson that he would be picked by the A's that he "crossed" them, working out a code with his catcher, Chief Meyers, by which he would call the pitches and his catcher would throw up phony signals.

Even if the Van Zelst rumor was unfounded, it was part of the head game that the Athletics played, keeping their opponents off balance with the threat of an undetectable spy system. "Personally," Mathewson wrote, "I do not believe that Connie Mack's players steal as much information as they get the credit for, but the reputation itself, if they never get a sign, is valuable. If a prizefighter is supposed to have a haymaking punch in his left hand, the other fellow is going to be constantly looking out for that left." For their part the A's kept the guessing game going long after the Series was over. In January 1912 Harry Davis said in a *New York Times* interview, "Half our reputation in getting the other team's signal was a bluff. Any time we got three or four hits in an inning we would give the other team some hint that we were getting their signals. That threw them into the air and put them on the defensive. We worked that successfully on the Giants and they switched signals several times during the World Series." Davis, who had batted .197 in the 1911 regular season, added, "Once they changed signals just because I made a hit. They argued, I guess, that if old Harry Davis could get a hit he must know what was going to be pitched."[7]

But Mathewson himself admitted that the Giants had been outwitted by the Athletics. In the second game Marquard was pitching, and he began to get "World Series nerves." In the sixth inning, after two men were out, the Athletics' Eddie Collins smashed a two-base hit to left. He then took only a short lead off second base, for he was trying to discover Meyers's signals. A hit meant the game. Seeing what Collins was up to, Meyers walked out to the box and said to Marquard, "No matter what I signal for, you throw Baker two curve balls."

Then, to fool Collins, Meyers gave false signals. With two balls pitched, however, the supply was out, and, not daring to give a signal, Meyers put it up to Marquard. Marquard flashed back that he was going to throw a fast one. Collins knew his sign and flashed the news to Baker. As a result Baker was all set, and when the ball came across the plate he simply swung his bat and it went screaming over the right-field fence. Overanxious in the excitement of that swift moment, Marquard and Meyers forgot that Collins had been spying on our signs and knew what was coming. That is the authentic inside story of the first home run to make Baker famous.[8]

To this day there is no evidence that would show that the 1911 Series was stolen, or how. Louis Van Zelst passed away in 1915, never confirming or denying the allegations made about him. Clearly, though, Mack's head games had given the edge to his team. Mack would never talk about any of this. Many years later, in 1950, at the end of his career, he wrote a primer on baseball, *Connie Mack's Baseball Book*, and declared, "The object is to keep your signals secret so that your opponents won't get wise to them. For that reason, I am not going to cite examples of the Athletics' signals, nor am I going to disclose how much we know of our opponents' signals."[9]

Following the signal wars in the 1910–11 World Series, there was intense fan focus on the growing variety of signs and signals—or "wig-wagging," as it was almost always termed at this time. In 1913 Ed Goewey wrote in his baseball column in *Leslie's Illustrated Weekly*, "Of course, no two catchers use the same movements to sign for a certain ball, unless it be by accident. In fact, a dozen backstops might make exactly similar movements and yet each would call for a different pitch. The variety of signals which can be arranged with the hands and manner in which they are held against the legs are almost limitless."[10]

George Stallings, who managed in Boston from 1913 to 1920, made signal history with his teeth. A man of relatively dark complexion, his bright-white teeth could be seen from the dugout, where he apparently called plays by opening and shutting his mouth. The running gag was that Stallings's men missed signals only on days when their skipper forgot to clean his teeth. Catcher Chief Meyers often bucked the hand-signal trend and signaled his pitchers by touching his mask, often throwing finger signals as decoys.

Writers loved to discover instances in which errant signals spelled the difference between victory and defeat. Connie Mack allegedly won an unspecified game in Chicago by pulling his hat down to keep the sun out of his eyes; it was mistaken for a bunt sign, the bunt was successfully executed, and the A's won the game. In another story a manager slapped his forehead to kill a fly, triggering the hand-to-head steal signal for a runner on first. The results were a disaster, as the bases were full with one out, and the inadvertent sign retired the side.[11]

Sometimes reporters were let in on a team's signals that were then reported openly, suggesting the possibility that the reporter might be part of a disinformation campaign and that the report was a decoy for the real signals. One team let on to a reporter that it was the umpire's call that set the next pitch—fastball after a strike and curve after a ball, unless the catcher called for a switch. An American League team claimed that it set the hit-and-run play by the way the batter rubbed his hands in the dirt to get a better grip on the bat: if the rub was up and down or just down, there was no play, but if he rubbed up, the man on first knew what to expect.

Meanwhile, signs and signals became part of the show, with colorful coaches, such as Detroit's Hughie Jennings and Arlie Latham, starring on the sidelines. Hugh Fullerton described Jennings in action: "He doubles his fists, lifts one leg and shakes his foot, screams 'E-Yah!' in piercing tones and suddenly plucks at the grass, pecking at it like a hen."[12]

Coaches' boxes also became sites of espionage. In a story in the *New York Times* on January 24, 1913, Detroit Tiger president Frank Navin blamed the excessive length of the games on the "coachers' boxes." Navin, reacting to AL president Ban Johnson's complaint that too many 1912 games had taken two hours or more to play, said that the boxes should be moved back so that the catcher could give the pitcher his signals more quickly. From where they were, he said, the coaches could detect the catcher's signals unless extra time was taken to hide them. The boxes were not moved and remain in place today.

The only manager at Connie Mack's level during this period was John McGraw, skipper of the New York Giants from 1902 into part of the 1932 season. Counting his two years as managing the old Baltimore Orioles, his win-loss record over thirty-three years in baseball was 2,763-1,948. (Mack, on the other hand, managed for an incredible fifty-three years, compiling a regular season record of 3,731-3,948.)

McGraw allowed his players to signal one another when to steal: a runner on first could signal the batter he was about to steal, just as the batter could call for the runner to take off. Either the sender or the receiver had veto power if he thought the play would not work. "In 1911 we stole 347 bases," said Fred Snodgrass, who stole 51 of them. "Just the New York Giants—347 stolen bases in one season! Look it up, if you don't believe it. And most of the time we ran on our own."[13]

McGraw, of course, often would call a play. In fact, he used a multitude of signals in directing his team, including things that came naturally. He once told an interviewer that his favorite signal was "blowing his nose," and his players said that "a nod" of his head was also common.

During the first decade of the twentieth century, when Luther "Dummy" Taylor was one of the Giants' leading pitchers, McGraw came up with a variation on hidden language. Taylor was a deaf-mute who took it as an affront if one did not learn sign language. Everyone, including McGraw, learned to converse with Taylor. Depending on his mood, McGraw managed from either the third base coach's box or the bench, and he sometimes spelled out simple instructions to all his players, such as S-T-E-A-L or B-U-N-T, in sign language. For his part, Taylor seemed to be able to "read" situations that others missed. His 1958 obituary in the *New York Times* commented that "sports writers of Mr. Taylor's time observed that he gave up few stolen bases, as he could divine a base runner's intention instantly by the facial expressions of the runner, the coaches and other players on the field."[14]

At times McGraw became autocratic about calling plays. In the midst of a home run spree, with five homers in a week, Mel Ott came to bat at a point when hitting away seemed appropriate, but, in glancing at the dugout, he saw that McGraw was flashing him the bunt sign. Ott couldn't believe his eyes and, stepping out of the box, looked back at McGraw, who again flashed the bunt sign. The same pantomime was repeated twice more, finally causing McGraw to stride out of the dugout and bellow, "Do you dare question McGraw?" Ott bunted.

An incident in the 1913 World Series underscored the power of a misunderstood signal. On offense the Giants positioned coach Wilbert Robinson at first base, while manager McGraw put himself at third. Fred Snodgrass, who was lame with a charley horse, singled at a crucial point in what was to be the last game of the Series. Snodgrass picked up a real or imagined steal sign and started hobbling off to second base on his bad leg, where he was thrown out by twenty feet by an incredulous Philadelphia Athletics catcher.

McGraw and Robinson, until then business partners and life-long friends, got into a fierce argument after McGraw upbraided Robinson for sending Snodgrass, and Robinson countered that he was simply relaying the skipper's steal sign. McGraw denied giving any sign. The game was lost and so, eventually, was the Series, with Connie Mack's Athletics again besting the Giants, this time four games to one.

The two old friends took the savage dispute from the ball-park to a saloon party held on the night of the last game of the Series for former members of the original Baltimore Orioles. Deep into a night of heavy drinking, in which McGraw chided Robinson for both the Snodgrass signal as well as other coaching errors, Robinson retorted that McGraw had made more mistakes during the Series than everyone on the team put together. The evening ended with McGraw throwing Robinson out of the party, according to umpire Bill Klem, who was there. Robinson tossed a glass of beer on his boss on the way out. Some said he was fired on the spot, but whether he was or not, Robinson became manager of the Brooklyn Dodgers the next season. The two did not speak again for many years and then only as team officials—as Hall of Fame historian Lee Allen put it, "For eighteen more years, they would glare at each other from opposing dugouts."[15]

If this public dispute was damaging to McGraw and his Giants, it was minor compared to what *Baseball Magazine* later called "a substantial factor" during the Athletics' 1913 championship season. The assertion made by the magazine's James Crusinberry was that "the high honor attained by Connie Mack's team was gained as much through its skillful manipulation of a signal tipping system as through its heavy batting and strong pitching, and what I have to say on this matter will be corroborated in general by every manager and player in the American League and many in the National League who have come into contact with Mack's team."

Once again Mack had used his coaches and players to pick pitches before they were thrown. It seems that teams all over the game were talking about the A's ability to get their signs, and no matter how many times they changed them, they seem to get solved. Crusinberry pointed out that some "careless action on the part of the infielder or some little habit of the pitcher" was what tipped off the A's. Mack's control of his own club and his ability to spy on the other team were clearly without equal, though the full measure of his skill was not known for years to come, when his early players got older and felt it was safe to reveal their techniques.[16]

In 1930 "Bullet Joe" Bush, one of the best Athletics pitchers between 1913 and 1925 (he was forty-nine days short of his twenty-first birthday when he beat the New York Giants 8–2 in the 1913 World Series), announced in an article in the *Saturday Evening Post* that "stealing signs is a lost art in baseball," insisting that "all that counts now is the boom-boom of the bat." Bush was decrying the end of the first decade of the "Live Ball Era," which he felt was turning scorekeepers into "expert mathematicians."

To glorify the tactics of the past, Bush revealed many examples of players that he and his teammates had decoded over the years. His confederates in this were pitcher Chief Bender, first baseman Harry Davis, and outfielder Danny Murphy. The catalog of tips-offs included that of "Big Ed" Walsh, whom Bush regarded as the greatest spitballer ever, who gave up his intention to throw his "bewildering" pitch when the peak of his cap rose. Walsh would put the ball to his mouth for every pitch but open his mouth only when he transferred alum to the ball. Opening his mouth caused his hat to move. Cleveland spitballer Stanley Coveleski, by contrast, did not touch his mouth with the ball when a fastball was coming: the A's third base coach could see daylight between the ball and the pitcher's lips. Pitcher Jim Shaw of Washington betrayed himself during his windup, keeping his wrist straight for a fastball but bending it for a curve.

Hall of Famer Walter Johnson was a hard case to solve, but the A's finally got two great signals: he brought his pitching arm farther back for his famous fastball, and he never threw a curve, but always a fastball, when the count was 3-2. Catcher

John Henry, also of the heavily picked Washington team, did his best to hide his finger signals but unconsciously revealed himself when his right elbow moved whenever he called for a curveball.

Bush, of course, was making the point that sign-stealing had lost its importance because of the introduction of the live ball in 1920, a season in which Babe Ruth hit fifty-four home runs for the New York Yankees. His charge proved to be short-lived.[17]

4

The Magicians and Mimes
of the Live Ball Era

Perhaps no batter in the history of baseball was less affected by and more indifferent to signs than Babe Ruth. In 1919, the year before the start of the Live Ball Era and his last with the Boston Red Sox, Ruth hit a then record twenty-nine home runs. The following year he practically doubled that number, while slugging an astonishing .847, a record that stood for more than eighty years until broken by Barry Bonds in 2001 at .863. The Yankees, coincidentally, became the first team to draw one million paying customers to a ballpark, more than double the attendance of any other club to that point.

Not only was a new ball put into play in 1920, which the players insisted was livelier than its "dead ball" predecessor, but it was accompanied by the abolition of the spitball and other "trick" pitches. Seventeen spitballers were "grandfathered" into the new era, but for everyone else the trick pitch was illegal.

The year 1920 also saw the introduction of more new baseballs per game. Penurious owners who had previously kept misshapen, dirty balls in play for many innings—sometimes for a whole game—were forced to introduce more new balls per game, which meant they were generally easier to see and were livelier when hit. The event that dictated this change took place on the drizzly afternoon of August 16, 1920. Under conditions of low visibility, Yankees submarine pitcher Carl Mays loosed a muddy ball that struck Cleveland's Ray Chapman in the head, killing him. Umpires were ordered to break out shiny white baseballs, free of foreign substances, as often as they felt the old ball was looking the least bit scruffy. Batting statistics climbed.[1]

Ruth's brand of ball was not signal based. By the end of the decade he had hit more home runs than the three top producers collectively hit in each of the first two decades of the century put together. Harry Davis (67), Charlie Hickman (58), and Sam Crawford (57) hit 182 homers between 1900 and 1910, and Gavvy Cravath (116), Fred Luderus (83), and Frank Baker (76) tallied for 275 round-trippers between 1910 and 1919 for a two-decade total of 457. Between 1920 and 1929 Babe Ruth alone hit 467.

In fact, Ruth's most cherished dream after his playing days were over—managing a team—was crushed because he couldn't master signals in his role as first base coach for the Brooklyn Dodgers in 1938. Dodger shortstop and team captain Leo Durocher complained that Ruth forgot his signals walking from the dugout to the coach's box. "No wonder we're getting piled up on the bases," he said. Ruth's biographer Marshall Smelser confirmed Durocher's position, quoting H. G. Salsinger, "a friendly, detached observer," who said of Ruth's career-long problem with signs: "He never remembered them."[2]

The postscript to the Babe's Ruthian inability to recall and understand signs took place in March 1948, the year he died, when he made a trip to spring training and visited a Cardinals–Red Sox game in St. Petersburg. Ruth's old skipper Joe McCarthy was in his first year managing the Red Sox. In the middle of the exhibition game Ruth turned to Gerry Hern of the *Boston Post* and said, "McCarthy is still using the same old signs. How do you like that? Same old signs. He'll have to come up with some new ones when he plays the Yankees."[3] McCarthy by all accounts was one of the canniest signers in the history of the game, known for his ability to constantly change his signs and his systems of sending them. Ruth may have recognized McCarthy's signs were the same, but their meaning had long since changed.[4]

Ironically, Ruth may be best remembered for an unorthodox signal, his "called shot" in Game Three of the 1932 World Series. Did he or didn't he? Recently discovered film shows he did make a gesture of some sort, though interpretations differ as to what it actually meant. Ruth himself had trouble recalling what happened. Baseball journalist Jerome Holtzman concluded that Ruth had not pointed and even quotes Ruth's denial the following spring when broadcaster Hal Totten asked him if he had made the gesture: "Hell, no. Only a damn fool would do a thing like that." For a long time he was evasive when questioned, responding with, "Why don't you read the papers? It's all right there." As the legend grew, however, Ruth became more and more convinced that he had called his shot, but he also had constant prompting to help him with his notoriously poor memory.[5]

If the new era meant fewer offensive signals, it did not mean that batters had any less interest in knowing what the next pitch was going to be, and sign-stealing and looking for tip-offs remained prevalent. The first World Series of the new era proved this point.

In 1920 Burleigh Grimes, the great Hall of Fame spitball artist with the National League Brooklyn Dodgers (then still known officially as the Robins), displayed his remarkable abilities with a 23-11 record. Grimes was one of the seventeen grandfathered spitball pitchers. Brooklyn made it to the best-of-nine World Series, where they faced the Cleveland Indians. The Indians had overcome Chapman's tragic death to win the American League pennant by two games over the White Sox, who themselves suffered from a series of player suspensions meted out as a result of the "Black Sox" scandal of 1919.

Grimes won the second game 3–0, as the Indians were baffled by his spitter. During the game player-manager Tris Speaker of the Indians noticed something odd: Dodger second baseman Pete Kilduff was announcing each spitter by grabbing a handful of infield dirt. When any other pitch was thrown, Kilduff didn't pick up dirt. It was later revealed that Kilduff, who had come to the Dodgers late in 1919, had been having a problem handling Grimes's spitter. He had no trouble catching it, but it tended to slip out of his fingers when he threw it to first. So whenever Kilduff saw a spitball being called for by his catcher, he would reach for the dirt to counteract the slippery ball.

When the Indians next faced the great spitballer in the fifth game, neither Grimes nor Kilduff could figure out why the Indians were laying off the spitballs and hammering the dry pitches. The Dodgers lost the game by a margin of seven runs.

In the seventh game of the Series, down four games to two, Grimes got the start again after slated starter Rube Marquard was unable to appear because he had been arrested by Cleveland police for scalping tickets. Cleveland spitballer Stan Coveleski pitched his second shutout of the series, while Grimes gave up three runs. Sam Balter of the *Los Angeles Herald Express*, who later wrote about Kilduff's inadvertent gaff, said, "Burleigh Grimes the incomparable was never hammered so hard and so unmercifully as in this Series. His two defeats cost the Dodgers the world championship." By comparison Cleveland's much less heralded spitballer Coveleski finished with three wins.

Occasionally, a manager or coach found a new method of signing. In 1933, at the age of twenty-seven, Washington Senators shortstop Joe Cronin was appointed player-manager despite the fact that he knew little about pitching and confessed this to his catcher Luke Sewell. He asked Sewell to tell him when to warm up a reliever and bring in a new pitcher. The two worked out a system by which Sewell would throw dirt in various directions to let his skipper know what to do next. A few years earlier, when he won the World Series against Joe McCarthy's 1929 Cubs, Connie Mack signaled away with his famed scorecard, but all of the signs were decoys. The legitimate code came from a rookie positioned next to the water cooler.

Mack recognized that sign-stealing was facilitated by recently traded players carrying their former team's code with them. So when he traded third baseman Jimmy Dykes to the White Sox in 1933, Mack changed the meaning of all of his signals. In his first game against his former teammates, Dykes caught Mack's previous sign for a sacrifice bunt. As the pitcher wound up, Dykes charged the batter, who smashed a line drive just past his head for a double. "I almost forgot to tell you," Mack said from the dugout. "Since you left, we changed our signs." After the game Dykes came up to Mack tongue in cheek and said, "Gosh, Mr. Mack, things are coming to an awful state when we can't trust an old gentleman like you."

Having learned a lesson, Dykes, as a manager, was careful to change his signs when a player was traded, but when the White Sox traded Zeke Bonura to the Washington Senators in 1938 he decided not to because "Bonura never caught any of our signs when he played for us." In their first meeting of the 1939 season Bonura found himself on third in a tie game. Pondering the situation, Dykes stroked his chin, and Bonura took off for home. The startled Chicago pitcher threw wild, and Bonura scored the winning run. "I saw Dykes touch his chin and that's his sign to steal," said Bonura after the game. "I forgot I wasn't on his team any more."

Bill Terry, Giants manager from 1932 through 1942, ran a tight ship with a stern rule that his players had to learn the team's signs no matter how often they were changed. On July 1, 1934, Terry called a young bench warmer named Phil Weintraub into the game to face Dizzy Dean in the eighth inning with a runner on first base. Weintraub looked to his third base coach for a sign and stepped into the batter's box. Just as Dean was about to go into his windup, Weintraub stepped out of the box to get the sign again. He did this twice more, and as he stepped out for the fourth time, Dean rushed to the plate. "Come on, son. Hell, he's done give you the bunt three times. Let's go." This story was told many times in the following years and, in fact, became the central anecdote in manager Paul Richards's "Signs and Signals" section in his instructional *Modern Baseball Strategy*.

Two men in the 1930s and 1940s—Charlie Dressen and Del Baker—were particularly adept at stealing signs. Their abilities guaranteed each long careers in the game as decoders. Between them, as players, coaches, and managers, they may well have netted more than a hundred or more wins by applying their skills.

Dressen created a reputation for himself as a player-coach for the Minneapolis Millers of the American Association. In 1932 Dressen's team was hitting the top pitcher for the Columbus Blue Birds, Pete Fowler, to the extent that he seldom lasted more than an inning against them. Columbus owner Larry MacPhail couldn't figure it out, especially since Fowler was doing so well against the other teams in the league. "One day," MacPhail said later in 1936, "I was talking to Mike Kelley, president of the Minneapolis club. I remarked on the inability of Fowler to get by the first inning whenever he faced Minneapolis. Mike smiled. 'That's easy,' he said. 'Dressen was out there on the coaching lines, and he could tell from Fowler's actions on the mound just what he was going to pitch. . . . Our hitters knew what was coming so they took a toe-hold and just teed off.'"

MacPhail made a note then that Dressen might be working with him someday. He soon became the general manager for the Cincinnati Reds and in the midst of the 1934 season hired Dressen to lead the team out of the National League cellar. "In the three and a half seasons I managed Cincinnati there was never a game played where I failed to steal at least one sign," he told a reporter in 1939.[6]

As had been true in Minneapolis, Dressen had an uncanny ability to read the battery for telltale tip-offs. Although he was quick to claim his abilities, he was usually tight-lipped when it came to how he did it, only occasionally revealing an insight. Dressen once told sportswriter Bob Addie that he could often read catchers by the way they squatted: "Some catchers stretch that left leg out when they call for the curve to block a ball going into the dirt." As for shortstops, "They move toward second when a fast ball is called for on a right-handed hitter and toward third when it's a curve ball."

Dressen's specialty, however, was reading pitchers. "It all boils down to discovering whether they're planning fast ball or curve," he once explained. "Dazzy Vance used to flutter his fingers before a curve. Fritz Ostermueller dips down once for a fast ball, twice for a curve. Some pitchers twist their wrists to make a ball break; others hold fingers tightly against the seam—and I can see a seam a hundred feet away. Lots of guys check their grip with their eyes. I watch foot movements, notice that one dope sticks his tongue between his teeth, another lets his glove drop, exposing his curve. Whenever I catch on, I yell our private sign."[7]

Dressen could also decode other coaches and managers. On the eve of the 1937 All-Star Game, in the lobby of the Shoreham Hotel in Washington DC, Dressen met with the National League All-Stars, standing in for team manager Bill Terry, who would not arrive until a few hours before game time. Among other things, the players were worried about which signals would be used. "Don't give it a thought," Dressen told the assembled talent. "Just stick to the signs you use on your own teams. I'll give them to you; I know 'em all."[8]

Detroit manager Del Baker, whose team won the 1940 American League pennant, already had a reputation as a master signal snatcher when his skills were unexpectedly enhanced that season. "We won the pennant partially because of a freak thing in the early days of September," Hank Greenberg said in his autobiography. Third baseman Pinky Higgins was out of the lineup with an injury, and pitcher Tommy Bridges, who was his hunting buddy, had purchased a new rifle with a telescopic sight. One afternoon the day after Bridges had pitched and prior to the next game, the two men were sitting in the upper deck of the left-field pavilion, and Bridges was looking through the rifle's scope. "Sure enough," Greenberg reported, "he was able to see the catcher's signs to the pitcher and, being a pitcher himself, it wasn't long before he was able to determine what the pitch was going to be."

Before the season ended they had moved the operation several times and had switched to using binoculars, but the impact was dramatic and consistent. "Rudy York and I had a field day," remembered Greenberg. "Both of us were long-ball hitters who had to get that little extra on the swing to hit the ball out of the park, and it was tremendously helpful to know what the pitch was going to be. . . . As I remember it, between the two of us we hit one or two home runs for seventeen consecutive days during the month of September." Bob Feller, whose Indians lost the pennant by one game, for decades maintained that the binoculars "cost us the pennant." For his part, Baker was given the title of "Magician of 1940" by *The Sporting News* for beating the Yankees and the Indians.[9]

The World Series between Baker's Tigers and Jimmy Wilson's Cincinnati Reds proved that even Baker's legendary abilities had their practical limitations. They abandoned the binoculars for fear of discovery and violence to the man with the glasses. Birdie Tebbetts, catcher for Detroit, later recalled, "Our manager, Del Baker, one of the brainiest men in baseball, was a great sign-stealer. But in that World Series sign-stealing didn't help. We knew every pitch the Reds' pitchers were going to throw, yet lost. Catcher Jimmy Wilson was giving away the pitches by twitching his forearm muscles when he called a curve. When the muscles were still, the pitch was a fast ball."[10]

Tebbetts was fascinated by the tendency of catchers to give the crucial tip-off. In an article for the *Atlantic Monthly* in 1949, he wrote, "It is surprising how many major league catchers develop faulty habits which tip off pitches to the opposition. To protect himself a catcher must be absolutely sure that every movement he makes—after coming out of the sign-giving crouch—is exactly the same for every pitch." He went on to suggest a clever technique to assist the pitcher: "A right-handed pitcher who has a tendency to hang a curve ball may be helped by having the catcher shift his weight to the right just as the pitcher is about to release the ball. This shift of weight will make the pitcher realize the ball must be thrown with the catcher's shift, and to the catcher's new position. It also will help him to hold on to the ball long enough to correct the hanging of the ball."[11]

In May 1941 word got out through an article in *The Sporting News* that fastballer Bob Feller, in his sixth year with the Cleveland Indians and coming off a twenty-seven-win season, was telegraphing pitches to third base coaches around the league. They claimed that when a fastball was called by his catcher, he would wiggle his fingers. The story was assumed to be a setup devised to get Feller to think about his devastating fastball and perhaps upset his timing. This got back to Feller, whose response was "Any hitter dumb enough to rely on a sign from his third base coach is going to end up picking red stitches out of his ear."

If nothing else, the episode illustrates that even the canniest sign stealer has always flirted with disaster. During the late 1930s there were a number of cases in which a batter got hit because he was expecting a different pitch than the one thrown. In 1937 Mickey Cochrane, the Detroit player-manager, suffered a triple skull fracture that put him on the critical list for five days and ended his playing career. It was widely assumed that Cochrane had been given a bad signal by Del Baker, but Cochrane denied it, insisting that he lost track of the ball and it had sailed in on him. A similar incident occurred in 1940, when Joe Medwick was hit in the head by a pitch thrown by Bob Bowman of the St. Louis Cardinals after he had allegedly been incorrectly tipped by Dressen.

Yet even the best could get crossed. In 1947 Dressen found himself coaching at third for the Yankees when Joe DiMaggio was still in his prime. According to Bill James in his *Guide to Baseball Managers*, Dressen insisted that all batters be given "private signs," whether they wanted them or not. When DiMaggio insisted that he didn't want to know, Dressen said he would give him the signal anyhow but that DiMaggio could ignore it if he wanted. One time Dressen signaled a curve, and DiMaggio accepted it. When a fastball almost beaned him, he barked, "That's it. Knock it off before you get me killed."[12]

During Lou Boudreau's second year as the Cleveland Indians' player-manager, in 1943, he came down with a bad cold—sufficient to take him out of the lineup but not serious enough to take him out as manager—when an incident occurred that showed that sign givers as well as stealers could create problems. During the game the Indians had runners on first and second when Boudreau grabbed a towel from the bench with which he wiped his runny nose. Suddenly, both men, neither of whom was known for his speed, took off, giving the opposition an easy and unexpected double play. Boudreau yelled at third base coach Oscar "Spinach" Melillo for putting on such a foolish play. Melillo reminded Boudreau that he had called the play by putting a towel to his face.

Five years later, then a seasoned seven-year player-manager, Boudreau and the Indians were involved in an audacious sign-stealing scheme. At the heart of the plan were three future Hall of Famers, including player-manager Lou Boudreau and ace pitchers Bob Feller and Bob Lemon.

To pick up pitch signs from opposing catchers, the Indians employed a telescope that Feller had used as a gunnery officer on the uss *Alabama* during World War II. "I used it to pick up enemy aircraft coming in at us," Feller told Schneider. "It's only about three feet long, maybe a little less, about two and a half feet. I've still got it at my home." The telescope was mounted on a tripod, placed in the Cleveland scoreboard, and operated alternately by Feller or Lemon, who remembered that he "could see the dirt under the catcher's fingernails." They would call out the next pitch to a groundskeeper—brothers Marshall and Harold Brossard or their father, Emil—who would then use another opening in the scoreboard to relay the signs to Tribe hitters, by a variety of changing signals, from a space otherwise used to post numbers for out-of-town games. The signs changed often, so that on a given day an arm poking out of the hole might mean a curveball and a face peering out might mean a fastball.[13]

"Hey, all's fair in love and war, and when you're trying to win a pennant," said Feller, who admitted that he was "probably" the instigator of the spy ring, along with Boudreau, which began a few weeks into the season when the Indians discovered that bullpen spies in Detroit and Boston were spying on them. Other teams had a pretty good idea what the Indians were up to; on one occasion, as a home run hit off Joe Page landed in the seats, the whole Yankee bench jumped up and began pointing at the scoreboard.

The season came down to a one-game, winner-take-the-pennant playoff game. The Indians won playing in Fenway Park with Feller's telescope back in Cleveland, so it did not play a role in that final game. But Cleveland had gotten there with a major assist from a piece of military hardware. "The way I felt about it, it was like in the war," remembered Feller. "You had to decipher a code, break it down, which we did against the Germans and the Japanese, and we won, right."[14]

Participants insist that the practice stopped after the pennant was won. But Johnny Sain, the Boston Braves pitcher who lost Game Four of the World Series on Larry Doby's home run, was always convinced Doby knew what was coming. Doby insists he did not know the scheme was in play. The Indians won the Series 4–2.

With the postwar ascendance of relief pitching, a tradition of playful pantomime calls to the bullpen developed. It was a short-lived phenomenon, soon replaced by the expediency of the bullpen telephone and less creative managers, but it was fun while it lasted and, if nothing else, entertained the crowd.

One of the earliest practitioners of this minor baseball art was Connie Mack, who termed bullpen phones "newfangled nonsense." To summon Joe Coleman he had a coach stand in front of the dugout and mimic a man shoveling coal, while Dick Fowler was called by a coach bending over and pretending to pick flowers (Mack called him Mr. Flowers), and Carl Scheib was alerted by a coach beating his fists against the nearest wall of the stadium, Shibe Park.[15]

As manager in Brooklyn in the early 1950s, Charlie Dressen would go through the exaggerated motions of eating spaghetti to call Italian American Ralph Branca and of chugging a beer to call Hank Bierman. Cot Deal, who pitched for the Red Sox and Cardinals in the late 1940s and early 1950s, was summoned with a shuffle and a tossing of imaginary playing cards, while an imaginary face lathering was the call for Sal "the Barber" Maglie. Bespectacled relievers got the nod when their skipper or a coach put circled fingers around each eye, paunchy pitchers were summoned with a depiction of an exaggerated bay window, and tall relievers were notified with a hand held palm down high above one's head.

When *The Sporting News*'s Joe King did a late-1950s roundup of the custom, he found these signals among others: hands held high in an apparent shape of a church steeple for Bubba Church of the Phillies (also for Johnny Podres of the Dodgers because this was Walter Alston's idea of the shape of Podres's head); a circling motion of the fist was Alston's call for Clarence Churn; a rowing motion was White Sox Coach Johnny Cooney's call for Bob Shaw (as in rowing ashore), as well as Joe Gordon's for Riverboat Smith; while a hand against the face was Danny Murtaugh's logical call for popular reliever Elroy Face.[16]

Catcher Joe Garagiola became a student of these calls. Every time he was traded he enjoyed learning the bullpen messages of his new team. In 1954, the season after being traded to the Cubs, he was working the bullpen and saw a sign he had never seen before: a coach standing in front of the dugout holding his sides and going through the motions of laughing. Asking the bullpen coach what that meant, Garagiola was told, "They want you to get ready to catch."

As in so many other things in baseball, the topper belongs to Casey Stengel during his six-year stint as manager of the Boston Braves between 1938 and 1943. It was getting dark toward the end of a long Braves-Giants Sunday-afternoon doubleheader at the Polo Grounds when Stengel decided to change pitchers. Suddenly, two small piles of newspapers were blazing in front of the Braves dugout. Umpire Bill Klem ran over to give Stengel the thumb. "How can you throw me out?" he demanded. "I'm only using the Paul Revere signals we always use in Boston— one for a left-hander, two for a right-hander."

The demise of this colorful custom at the hands of the bullpen phone brought its own problems. Garagiola recalled, "Moe Drabowsky used to amuse himself by picking up the phone in his bullpen, calling the other bullpen, disguising his voice, and ordering certain pitchers to start warming up." While pitching for the Cubs, Drabowsky forced a momentary return to the old system. "I always had a penchant for getting on the phone," Drabowsky recollected.

In Milwaukee County Stadium, you can get an outside line in the bullpen. I was a stockbroker in the off-season, and I'd get an outside line and talk to some broker friends of mine. I was getting stock quotes one day. Poor Glen Hobbie [Cubs starting pitcher]. Here come Eddie Mathews, Hank Aaron, Frank Thomas. They're trying to get somebody to warm up in the bullpen. I'm sure the manager figured he must have gotten the wrong number. He kept getting "beep, beep, beep" on the phone. Then a couple guys get up in front of the dugout steps waving towels like semaphore signals. I was probably responsible for Hobbie's earned run average being higher than it should have been.[17]

5

A Golden Age for Cheaters, Stealers, and Scoreboard Spies

In February 1957 Ty Cobb granted an interview to *The Sporting News* in which he said that the plethora of signs being flashed to hitters was taking the bat out of their hands. "I think the batter should have the privilege of hitting the ball he wants, especially if there are men on the bases. Going after the first pitch, for instance, helps the element of surprise which you need in a tough game." Cobb's lament fell on deaf ears, for as sign-stealing proliferated, so did the complexity of the sign schemes themselves.[1]

"Stolen signs win a lot of ball games," said Dodgers vice president Fresco Thompson in 1952. It was conventional wisdom that any team hoping to contend needed a master in the art of sign-stealing. While Charlie Dressen and Del Baker got much of the attention, others were doing the same thing but with less fanfare. "Coochi is just as good a sign stealer as Dressen," Casey Stengel told Tom Meany, referring to Indians third base coach Tony Cuccinello in 1952, "but he never lets on about it, so you don't know what he's getting away with." Bill Veeck said he felt that Roxie Lawson, who stole for him at Milwaukee, was more effective than Dressen because he was not detected and could steal a sign and "let the glory go." He felt that the game's best stealers were as unknown as Lawson.[2]

The 1952 National League pennant was won by Dressen's Dodgers, but he may have helped give away the World Series to the Yankees, who won in seven games for their fourth championship in a row.[3] The Yankees were leery of Dressen's pilfering skill and watched his every move. He actually sneaked into Yankee Stadium near the end of the regular season to spy on the Yankees, anticipating the upcoming Series. According to John Lardner of *Newsweek*, "He put his binoculars to his eyes and, for several minutes, all he could see was a file of Yankee ushers goose-stepping in front of him, a gesture of welcome from the Yankee management." Fans sent him a cup of whiskey with the message "For the spy in the third row on the aisle," and then more than seventy-five "old friends" stopped by to say hello, including a man introducing himself as a Yankee spy, who asked him if he had "any secrets to share."[4]

In the fifth inning of the fourth game, the Dodgers were down one run and had men on second and third with pitcher Joe Black coming to bat. A squeeze bunt was logical, and the Yankees were watching for it. As was his custom, Dressen ran his team from the third base coach's box. With one ball and one strike on Black, second baseman Billy Martin intercepted Dressen's squeeze-bunt sign to the batter—a grab of his neck with his right hand tossed in amid a string of decoy signs— because the Dodger manager had carelessly flashed the same sign he had used as Martin's manager at Oakland in the Pacific Coast League several years before. Martin signaled the information to catcher Yogi Berra, who called for a pitchout from Allie Reynolds and tagged out the runner trying to score from third. The Yankees won to even up the Series, and for years Martin was eager to talk about outsmarting the man who claimed to be the best sign man ever.[5]

Part of the Yankees' success during the 1950s was connected to their ability to know what their opponents were about to do. Yogi Berra was among the best at calling games and keeping his signals secret, and he worked out a special system for calling Vic Raschi's pitches so they couldn't be deciphered. "We used scoreboard numbers which we added up and added to the sign I gave with my fingers to get the sign," he recently recalled. "Nobody could figure it out."[6]

Berra not only gave good signals but could pick them as well. Syd Thrift, Baltimore Orioles vice president of baseball operations—who had, as a young man, signed with the Yankees organization in 1949 and been assigned to their farm team in Amsterdam, New York—recalled in a 2002 interview, "The St. Louis Browns had a pitcher named Ned Garver who was a big winner on a bad team. One day Yogi Berra came back to the bench and said he had gotten Garver's signs in the on-deck circle in a day game. He could tell by the catcher's hand as it shadowed on the ground whether it was going to be a fast ball or a curve. Stengel said here is a guy who is supposed to be dumb, but boy is he smart."

On offense Berra claimed he had little interest in picked signs: "I wouldn't take a sign if their own catcher sent it to me Western Union," Berra announced in 1962. But he also watched his own pitchers for telltale mannerisms, which he worked to eliminate. "I read my own pitchers. They give away their pitches more often than not."

The Yankee players were adept at reading pitchers as well. "Some pitchers stop halfway in their windup when they're curving and r'ar back harder when they fast ball you," Mickey Mantle told a reporter. "Early Wynn throws everything but his knuckler from behind his head. The knuckler, he stops at his forehead and throws."[7]

Perhaps no pitcher in the history of baseball ever adapted better to the knowledge he was tipping his pitches than Don Larsen. On October 8, 1956, in Game Five of the World Series, Larsen pitched a perfect game against the Brooklyn Dodgers— the first perfect game in the 307-game history of the World

Series and the first in a Major League game since April 30, 1922, an extraordinary feat for a pitcher who two seasons before had been a 21-game loser with the Baltimore Orioles.

Often forgotten in the retelling of this singular moment was that Larsen pitched the whole game without benefit of a wind-up—as if he had faced all twenty-seven Dodgers with a runner on first. Minutes after the win Larsen explained that during the latter days of the season, he learned he was tipping his pitches to Del Baker, then a coach for the Red Sox. "No matter what I threw Baker knew in advance what was coming," he said. Larsen went to Yankee pitching coach Jim Turner and told him that he wanted to drop his windup and adopt an unorthodox no-windup delivery. The results were sensational. Larsen's perfect game became a case study for others, and the lesson was clear: the simpler the delivery system, the less likely it was to be analyzed and deciphered by men like Baker.[8]

The old-fashioned hand-operated scoreboards continued to be a refuge for scouts, former players, and even staff from the front office. "We used to have our traveling secretary up in the scoreboard stealing signs," the Cubs' Moe Drabowsky confessed. "Don Beebe was his name. You've got all the little squares in the scoreboard and he'd be sitting way back in the squares. If he put his foot in the right-hand corner, that meant fastball. The hitter would just look up toward the pitcher and look past him at the scoreboard and see the squares, and if he *sees* a foot, he's ready to jump on a fastball. We might score nine runs or so and then lose 12–9, 13–10."[9]

Periodically, someone would complain that they were being spied upon by men out of uniform hanging out in the scoreboard, and they would be answered by the official equivalent of a shrug and a scowl. For instance, on June 23, 1956, the *New York Times* carried the story that Baltimore Orioles manager Paul Richards, who had just been swept in four games at Comiskey

Park, had lodged a formal complaint with American League president Will Harridge that the White Sox were stealing signs with the aid of a scoreboard telescope. Harridge replied that there was no rule against sign-stealing. *Sports Illustrated*, in effect, mocked Richards, observing that there was no rule prohibiting the practice "against stealing signals, even if they are stolen by a man in a long black beard carrying a brass telescope," and that Harridge had stood up for fun and color, adding, "It was a blow to Richards but not to the fan who revels in these odd marginal disputes and who may, next time he sees a ball game, try to signal some signals himself." To help their readers, *Sports Illustrated* ran a pictorial on signs and how one might learn to pick them from one's seat.[10]

Organized baseball finally did react to an external device in 1959 but, in the end, attempted to restrict the use of only one particular space-age instrument and fell short of actually banning it.

On July 13, 1959, NBC broadcast its game of the week, between the Yankees and Red Sox, using its new Bushnell Spacemaster eighty-inch telephoto lens. It could show the catcher's fingernails from four hundred feet, and the two announcers on the local version of the broadcast shown in New York with the NBC feed, Mel Allen and Phil Rizzuto, gleefully called each pitch before it was thrown by the Red Sox pitcher. One of the viewers happened to be Commissioner Ford Frick, who decided that such exposure was a bad idea and immediately got NBC to agree not to use the lens again and instructed the owners of all teams in both leagues that any contracts with television stations should be written to exclude the use of the eighty-inch lens.[11]

Yet baseball continued to look the other way with respect to other high-powered optical devices. Hank Greenberg, by then a co-owner with Bill Veeck of the Chicago White Sox, said in his autobiography that he knew it was going on during the White Sox's successful 1959 drive for the American League pennant.

"We stole the signs from the centerfield scoreboard, and I'm sure a lot of other ball clubs do the same," he wrote later. "As a matter of fact, it's rumored that the Yankees were stealing signs from their centerfield scoreboard for years. Know that they had a lot of success against Bob Feller. A lot of the hitters who didn't figure to hit Feller had good records against him, and I'm sure they were helped by knowing what was being pitched to them."[12]

A year later Bill Veeck introduced the exploding scoreboard at Chicago's Comiskey Park. The term and the concept were inspired by a pinball machine hitting the jackpot during the finale of William Saroyan's 1939 play, *The Time of Your Life*. The new scoreboard was great show business, and even when it didn't work or shot flaming debris onto the diamond, it made news—SHOOTING SCOREBOARD STRAFES CHICAGO INFIELD was an Associated Press (AP) headline—and it seemed to be emblematic of a happy-go-lucky owner and an organization that saw baseball as entertainment.[13]

What was not known but only suspected at the time was that the scoreboard housed a sign-stealing operation led by Dizzy Trout and that pitches were signaled with the flashing of a little red light in the right-hand corner, almost invisible among the pyrotechnics. This scheme so upset one man, Al "Red" Worthington, that he left the team and quit the game, albeit for only two years. Veeck did not comment on the matter until his memoir was published in 1962, at which time he said that Worthington was "a very religious man" who quit the club because "he thought we were playing unfair."[14]

Although the Worthington matter was kept fairly quiet when it happened, many other charges of sign-stealing from beyond the confines of the diamond were made that year. Several teams claimed that the Milwaukee Braves, then managed by Charlie Dressen, were getting catchers' signs from a coach with binoculars in the Milwaukee bullpen. The first complaint came from Gene Mauch of the Phillies in May, and on June 3 umpire Jocko Conlan went out to the bullpen and told the players and coaches hanging over the fence to sit down. Conlan had been told by the Cardinals, who had played there earlier in the season, that the group at the fence included a man with a spyglass. The Braves denied this, but they had a much harder time denying an incident in early July that took place in Chicago.[15]

"I watched the Braves do it out of the bleachers at Wrigley Field—up in the right center-field bleachers," said Don Zimmer, then a Chicago infielder. "We caught 'em one time. It happened to be Bob Buhl and Joey Jay. They had overalls and hats on, and finally somebody spotted 'em with binoculars from our bench and when they noticed that we had 'em spotted, they ran like hell." *Sports Illustrated* reported that "most National Leaguers say they doubt that Dressen knew anything about the spying," then asked tongue in cheek, "Wonder where he thought Buhl and Jay were spending the afternoon?"[16]

The incident prompted Cubs vice president John Holland to tell *The Sporting News*, without the slightest hint of indignity, "We haven't made any protest to the Braves and we won't. After all, there isn't anything in the rules against it." But the incident did have an effect on one longtime practitioner, the Cubs' first-year manager, Lou Boudreau, who was in his sixteenth and last year of managing. "Every ball club has done it one time or another," he announced, "but I am never going to resort to it again. I have a son [Lou Jr., thirteen] I'm trying to teach good sportsmanship, fairness and honesty. Somehow those spying tactics smack too much of cheating." Boudreau admitted that he had practiced scoreboard spying in Cleveland and that the Buhl-Jay incident was not the first transgression of the season against the hapless Cubs.[17]

At the end of the year *Baseball Digest* ran an article by Robert L. Burnes titled "Sign-Stealing by Remote Control? It's Overrated!" It contained an interview with an unnamed former player, manager, and coach who disputed the many stories about men with field glasses stealing signs from various locations outside the outfield fence. "I think it's all pure bunk. I don't think there's been a sign stolen by a spyglass this year or for a long time." Why, then, did the source refuse to reveal his identity? "It might give me a bad reputation with the coaches who like people to think they're always swiping signs."[18]

Lacking anything that would suggest satire, the interview can only be seen as one man's attempt to put a reverse spin on something that was out of control. The article was also ironic in that the 1961 season was notable for the number of sign-stealing accusations. In early May the Cubs alleged that the Cardinals had been stealing signs from the left-field scoreboard, and after other allegations during the summer, the episodes were capped when Milwaukee's new manager, Birdie Tebbetts, who had replaced Dressen, played a September 4 game under protest because the Cubs were stealing signs from their scoreboard, an almost comic reversal of the Buhl-Jay incident from the previous summer.[19]

Sign-stealing was becoming so sordid, so widespread, and such an embarrassment to the game that Major League Baseball (MLB) even flirted with the idea of banning the practice during the winter of 1961–62 but stopped short of drawing a clear line in the sand. However, the gloves came off in 1962, incited by an article that appeared in *True* magazine, a periodical of the time with a penchant for insider exposés. Entitled "You've Got to Cheat to Win in Baseball," it was written by Rogers Hornsby and a writer named Bill Surface.

Hall of Famer Hornsby has been called the greatest right-hand hitter in baseball history and had the numbers to support such a claim: in the successive years of 1921–25 his batting averages were .397, .401, .384, .424 (a modern record), and .403. Arthur Daley of the *New York Times* called this "the most unbelievable period of batting greatness in baseball history." He was also one of the game's angriest, most outspoken stars. One writer characterized him as "a liturgy of hatred." Hornsby managed five Major League Baseball clubs and was dismissed from each as the result of disagreement—mostly with the front office but also with his players.

Hornsby's article was a stunner. It opened this way: "When Al Worthington quit the Chicago White Sox last summer and went home to Alabama, most of the newspapers said it was a salary argument. In my book it wasn't. In my book he was a baseball misfit—Worthington didn't like cheating."

Hornsby then declared: "I've been in pro baseball since 1914 and I've cheated or watched someone on my team cheat. You've got to cheat." He offered a lengthy list of illegalities—alleging, for example, that 95 percent of all pitchers cheated and that the other 5 percent simply hadn't figured out how to—and pronounced Don Hoak the best cheating infielder in the game because of his ability to hold runners by their belts without getting caught. He said that certain players—Eddie Stanky, for one—could not have played in the Majors without cheating. Hornsby said Stanky wore heavily starched shirts with oversize sleeves that allowed him to lean over on a close pitch and seem to get "nicked." Hornsby added that Stanky had "plenty of other cute tricks."

Hornsby talked of scoreboard cheating as the norm and invoked at least one scheme that had not been made public before—a massive Indian head with moving eyes in an ad for Uneeda Water in the Detroit outfield. The eyes were moved to signal signs stolen from the scoreboard. When the Indian's eyes moved sideways, it was a curve; when they moved down, it was a changeup; and if they did not move, it was a fastball.[20]

The Hornsby exposé warmed up the Hot Stove League in the winter of 1962, setting the stage for an unprecedented spring training season during which much dirty laundry would get aired.

6

1962—the Year of the Revisionist Finger-Pointers

When the National League held its annual meeting in December 1961, the matter of complaints against sign-stealing teams came under consideration. National League owners gave their president, Warren Giles, the authorization to declare forfeit of any game won with signs obtained by mechanical means if such a transgression could be proven. The use of binoculars and telephones had never been deemed illegal, and this decision also fell shy of banning the practice. As Dan Daniel commented in *The Sporting News*, "In short, absolute evidence is impossible to obtain, even if it were to come from leakers who had been connected intimately with the operation."[1]

Hornsby's article ensured that the propriety of using a mechanical device to steal signals would be in the news when the first players reported to spring training in late February 1962. Hornsby arrived in Florida as the first batting coach for the New York Mets (still called the Metropolitans when he was hired) in their rookie season under Casey Stengel. He also brought with him his just-published book, aptly titled *My War with Baseball*, which he had also written with Bill Surface and contained a preface by Stengel and an expansion on the spying charges made in the *True* magazine article.[2]

My War with Baseball gave anyone with reason to dislike Hornsby added ammunition and made organized baseball, trying to sell itself as family entertainment, shudder.³ Although the book did not sell well, it touched nerves during spring training. Hornsby called Roger Maris, who had just come off his record-breaking sixty-one-home-run season, merely a right-field pull hitter who had the advantage of the short right field at Yankee Stadium. He accused American League pitchers of not pitching smart to Maris, throwing him too many inside pitches, which were, according to Hornsby, "all he was looking for so he can pull the ball." He said Maris would never compare to Babe Ruth. "He couldn't hit .400 if he added all his averages together," sneered Hornsby.

On the twenty-second of March at a Mets-Yankees game at St. Petersburg, a few days after the book had been published, a photographer attempted to get the two men together for a photograph. When Hornsby and the photographer approached Maris, he turned his back and began signing autographs for fans in the stands. Hornsby stormed off toward the nearest reporter, shouting, "What do you think of that bush leaguer. . . . He refused to pose with me. He couldn't carry my bat. He didn't hit in two years what I hit in one."⁴

A chapter in *My War with Baseball* also brought sign-stealing front and center, for Hornsby asserted again that the game was awash in cheaters. Hornsby made good copy. In one of several interviews he described a system that was "the way most teams have been doing it for years," which involved signaling through the zeros posted for scoreless innings. "When it's open that's a fast ball; closed is a curve, and half-open it's a change-up."⁵

Two days before the Hornsby-Maris confrontation, United Press International (UPI) ran a story the centerpiece of which was a charge made by pitcher Jay Hook that the Cincinnati Reds had won the 1961 National League pennant with the aid of scoreboard spies swiping the rival catchers' signs. Hook had been with the Reds the previous year and was now with the Mets and said that he had gone public because "I want to protect the Mets against that sort of thing. I think it's wrong."

Hook accused various Cincinnati personnel, including scout Brooks Lawrence, of spying from the walk-in hand-operated Crosley Field scoreboard with a set of binoculars and phoning in the purloined information to the dugout. Lawrence, a veteran of the Negro Leagues and the National League, said not only was it not done, but it couldn't be done. Lawrence said that he used to step into the scoreboard before games to smoke and that "you couldn't see anything," pointing out that the left center-field scoreboard was so situated that right-handed batters blocked the view of the catcher. Cincinnati manager Fred Hutchinson responded dismissively, pointing out, "That's Hook's story. He's stuck with it."[6]

Reacting to the Hook revelation, Leonard Schecter of the *New York Post* wrote an article titled "The Fiend with Glasses" in which he said that nothing was as disturbing to a pitcher than a "fiend abroad in the ball park with a pair of field glasses" picking up the catcher's signs. He likened a batter who knew what was coming to "the driver who knocks down an 89-year-old pedestrian. It's easy but unsporting."[7]

The Reds story became public some seventy-two hours before UPI's rival the Associated Press broke an even bigger one. Highly respected writer Joseph Reichler, quoting an unidentified former member of the New York Giants and at the time with another Major League team, claimed that the 1951 Giants had an electrician install a wire leading from the center-field clubhouse to the dugout. As signals were stolen with the aid of binoculars, a button was pushed and a buzzer rang in the dugout—one buzz for a fastball and two for a breaking pitch. The information was then relayed to the batter by a bench coach. The story claimed the Giants had used this "ingenious" system for the last three months of the 1951 season, during which time they had won thirty-six of the last forty-five games, overcoming the Dodgers' seemingly insurmountable thirteen-and-a-half-game lead and, with Bobby Thomson's home run, winning the National League pennant.[8]

The most stunning allegation in the story was that the prime beneficiary of this scheme had been Thomson himself and that his pennant-winning home run—forever a part of baseball lore as the final element in "The Miracle of Coogan's Bluff"—was aided from center field. (Footnote: "The home run was chosen as the greatest moment in baseball history by *The Sporting News* and by Dave Anderson of the *New York Times* as "arguably baseball's single most historic moment.")

"You might say," said the anonymous informant, "that the shot heard 'round the world was set off by a buzzer." When the story appeared the next day, the *Washington Post*'s headline for the AP story put it directly: SIGN-STEALING WITH BINOCULARS SET UP THOMSON'S FLAG WINNING HOMER, while the *New York Herald Tribune* headlined it CLUBHOUSE SPY HELPED THOMSON HIT HOMER IN '51, SAYS EX-GIANT.

Thomson's reaction was swift. He went on record in a follow-up AP story denying he had received any signals. "It was a high inside fastball and nobody called the pitch." Calling the charge "the most ridiculous thing I have ever heard of," he added, "If I'd been getting the signals, why wouldn't I have hit the first pitch? It was a fat one right down the middle." Ralph Branca backed up Thomson in the same wire-service story. "The first one was right down the pipe. On the second one, I tried to brush him back a bit but I didn't get the ball in tight enough. I always figured he just outguessed me."[9]

Thomson challenged the man who had made the charge "to show some character" and to come out in the open. Others chimed in to dispute the charge that the historic homer came on a stolen sign. Whitey Lockman, the Giant on second base when the home run was hit, said, "I couldn't even see Rube Walkers [the Dodger catcher] signal to Branca on that homer."

Alvin Dark (by then the manager of the San Francisco Giants), catcher Wes Westrum, and Willie Mays—all members of the '51 Giants—stated that the accusation against Thomson was completely baseless. Significantly, none of the players involved denied the spy operation, but they were adamant about Thomson not getting the signal. Mays told Jerry Liska of the Associated Press, "I was next up after Thomson, and if there was any sign stealing, I wasn't in on it."[10]

Dark may have been the most emphatic. From the Giants' spring training site in Phoenix, he said, "Anybody who knows anything about baseball knows that with a runner on second base no catcher in the business would give just one sign and stick with it. He flashes three or four phony signs. It would take either a genius or a very lucky man to select the legitimate sign and flash it to the hitter." Leo Durocher, who had managed the 1951 Giants and was a Dodger coach in 1962, was the only one to absolutely deny a system had been in use, declaring, "If we had signals Bobby would have murdered that first pitch."[11]

For their part, the 1951 Dodgers seemed no less impressed than the Giants by the revelation and just as sure in their defense of Thomson. Gil Hodges and Duke Snider said that they had heard rumors of the sign-stealing operation during the latter days of the season, and Hodges had been told for sure after the playoff by "a fellow who had good information." However, Snider and others insisted that even if the Giants had such a system, it was not effective. "If the Giants were stealing the Dodger signs, why didn't they steal them the day before the Thomson homer?" The day before they had lost to Clem Labine, 10–0.[12]

Branca was quoted in a follow-up story still insisting that a stolen sign had nothing to do with Thomson's pennant-winning home run. The *Los Angeles Times* quoted Branca saying, "The irony is that Rube Walker caught me that day [instead of Roy Campanella]. Rube used a different series of signals. Thomson didn't get advance notice of that pitch, but the Giants did get quite a lot that season." Another story quoted Branca from a local television interview saying that he learned of the scheme from pitcher Ted Gray in 1953, when both men were at Detroit, and that it was confirmed later when he was told by New York Giants pitchers Alex Konikowski and the very religious man who had left Bill Veeck's White Sox for moral reasons, Al Worthington. None of these people would have any real way of knowing. Gray never played for the Giants. Worthington did not reach the Majors until 1953, and Konikowski pitched a grand total of four innings for them in 1951.

Columnist Jack McDonald of the *San Francisco News & Call Bulletin* wrote, "No responsible wire service should dredge up a yarn after more than 10 years without pinning it on someone." McDonald had Thomson's personal assurance that it was untrue and also gave his own eyewitness account. "We saw the game. Thomson didn't indicate advance knowledge of the first pitch when he took a home run cut at the ball and missed it by a good foot. He then hit a high inside pitch off Ralph Branca for the shot that made history. Russ Hodges, the radio broadcaster, got so excited he still hasn't told his listeners what happened."[13]

"Right after the game," McDonald explained, "as we entered the Dodger clubhouse, Mgr. Charlie Dressen was carrying on like a raving maniac, shouting that if Branca had pitched where the catcher asked for the ball, Thomson would never have hit it." Dressen, who prided himself as a great sign stealer, gave no indication that his sign had been stolen but rather insisted that it had been ignored by his own pitcher.[14]

During the spring of 1962 reporters were regaled by veterans with other hitherto unknown transgressions. Phillies manager Gene Mauch boasted of a time when he was with the Dodgers for part of the 1948 season and, because he had a bad back, got the job of stealing signs from the visitor's center-field clubhouse at the Polo Grounds. Watching from the window and using binoculars to steal the catcher's signs, Mauch would place a peach-nectar can, large enough to be seen from the plate, in a window of the center-field clubhouse. If it was on the left side of the sill, the pitch was going to be a curveball; if on the right side, a fastball; and if in the middle, a changeup. Like many other insiders, Mauch said that the distinction between stealing from second base and the outfield was "cutting it kind of fine."[15]

Half a dozen related stories prompted by the allegations against the Giants appeared in *The Sporting News* on April 4, 1962. Taken as a whole, they seemed to concede that this was just another chapter in an ongoing saga dating back to 1876—in fact, the stories ran under the heading DANIEL TRACES SIGNAL-SWIPING HISTORY TO '76. The articles supported Hornsby's assertion that everyone did it. Marty Marion said he installed a scoreboard spy when he managed the White Sox in the mid-1950s. "I think Cleveland was pretty brazen about it," Marion added, "when Bob Feller would walk out to the bull pen carrying binoculars over his shoulder." Fred Haney, who had managed for ten years in the Majors, told Jack McDonald: "There's such a thing as being too smart in this game. . . . If anybody used the scoreboard to spy on my club when I managed the Braves it never got to me, but I'd have welcomed it. Look, you can get the signals in advance and there won't be more than a couple of hitters on any club that it will help."

The anonymous informant on the 1951 Giants also reported to Joe Reichler that a sign-stealing scheme had been in operation in 1959, the year the Dodgers beat out the Giants in the last week of the season. The informant had been with the Giants in 1959 and alleged that a former Giant coach was given the job of spying at a moment when the Giants led the league with the Dodgers in hot pursuit. "We used a more simple method in 1959," the informant recalled. "One fellow worked from the scoreboard. He kept two slats open. When the pitch was to be a fastball, he closed the right slat. For a curve he closed the left one."[16]

This time, however, the system was abandoned after only two days, on the eve of the Dodgers' arrival in town. According to this story, one of the Giants, described as "deeply religious," went to the manager and said he would "spill the works" unless the immoral system was abandoned. The Dodgers swept the series and took over first place. "I always thought we would have won the pennant if we had kept the spy system," he added. The Dodgers and Braves ended the season in a tie, with the Dodgers going on to win the playoffs and World Series. The Giants finished third.

Who was the informant? Nowhere did Reichler claim he was with the Giants in 1951, though he was clearly with the club in 1959 and "with another club" at the time of the 1962 Fort Lauderdale interview, although it does not say in what capacity. The man most likely to fit the description is Al Worthington, who was a pitcher for the Giants from 1953 to 1959.[17]

A few weeks after Hornsby's book was published, *Baseball Monthly* released an article by Jimmy Piersall, then an outfielder for the Washington Senators, who had recovered from the mental illness that had derailed his career. The piece, titled "How the Home Team Cheats," handled the allegations against the 1951 Giants and 1961 Reds matter-of-factly and went on to reveal other schemes, stating that virtually every part of the ballpark was rigged. "In Milwaukee, for example, the Braves bullpen crew enjoys bright clean lights for warming up. The visiting team's pitchers have only a single dim bulb to see what they are doing."[18]

Bill Veeck's autobiography appeared soon after and celebrated schemes he had devised, including moving the fences in or out by as much as fifteen feet, depending on who was coming to town; contouring the mound to unsettle visiting pitchers; employing creative interpretations of the weather to call rainouts in his favor; and, of course, stealing signs from the scoreboards. He retold the story of Worthington's leaving the team and commented, "And yet I doubt there is one team which had not tried it in recent years. There is absolutely nothing in the rules against it."[19]

Although much of what Hornsby and Veeck revealed was old hat to insiders, it was now much more public than ever before. Nonetheless, despite the comments made by Giles and other officials, by the summer no further action had been taken against sign-stealing, and the assertion stuck that it was not against the rules of the game. "Nowhere have I been able to find a rules reference to this sort of thing, a regulation banning it, officially," wrote Dan Daniel in *The Sporting News*. Indeed, when Commissioner Ford Frick was presented with some of the stories that spring, he merely asserted, "I am definitely opposed to such practices. If such a charge were substantiated, I would forfeit the game, but I would have to have evidence. I certainly would not be guided by rumor."

In late June Braves manager Birdie Tebbetts, who admitted that he had relayed signs from the scoreboard in Cleveland in an interview with Arthur Daley of the *New York Times*, lashed out at the system of scoreboard cheating, claiming it was actually "getting worse" and that the only one who could stop it was the commissioner. Tebbetts said, "If you believe in the integrity of the game the way I do, this practice has to stop. It's cheating. And cheating is just as contemptible in baseball as it is anywhere else."

The Braves' Lew Burdette and Warren Spahn, two of the era's greatest pitchers, also complained that one of the reasons games were dragging on for such a long time—perhaps as long as an extra half hour per game—was that, as Spahn put it, "we have to use complicated signs and disguise the real ones with meaningless sets in order to try to confuse the sign stealers." Daley ended his column with a demand: "If Tebbetts is correct— and he usually is—the cheating practice is spreading. It's time somebody in authority brought it to an abrupt halt." Tebbetts was the ideal voice of reason, a "baseball man" who had come into the game as a mascot for the Minor League Nashua (NH) Millionaires; spent fourteen years as a catcher for the Tigers, Red Sox, and Indians; and been a manager for another seven seasons and would continue to manage for another four. Tebbetts had managed for one of the worst offenders, Cincinnati; was now managing a second, Milwaukee; and would be hired to manage a third, the Indians, later in 1963.[20]

In the weeks following the article, there was a sudden end to baseball stories with the words "binocular" or "scoreboard spy" in them. An unwritten rule had somehow been instituted without benefit of an official ruling, to the effect that this had gotten out of hand and was now taboo. Perhaps Daley's influence as a journalist had been felt; perhaps it had been accomplished by quiet fiat from the top or been passed along from manager to manager as a "gentleman's agreement," maybe during batting practice or postgame dinners.

Under the new unwritten rules the only way one could steal signs from a point beyond the outfield fence was to be in uniform in the bullpen and to use the naked eye. Angels manager Buck Rodgers observed, "One of the best I ever saw at it was Don Lee [a pitcher with the Los Angeles Angels and five other teams in the early 1960s]. His eyesight was so good that he could stand in the bull pen at Cleveland and steal signs. He'd put his hand on the fence if it was one pitch and take it off if it was another. Sounds impossible, but he was able to do it. I was there. I was a beneficiary."[21]

Another legacy of the "spy-in-the-scoreboard" period in baseball history was that catchers' signs became much more sophisticated and harder to steal. If, as Rogers Hornsby and others insisted, everyone was doing it, then any club worth its salt was also working to protect their signs and signals. Pioneered by such managers as Leo Durocher and Paul Richards and clever catchers like Joe Garagiola and Yogi Berra, a new signing vocabulary was developed based on pumps, flaps, and flips, as well as the traditional system of flashing signals. The pump system was, and still is, based on the number of signs given rather than the signs themselves, so the real signal might be the fourth in the first inning and the fifth in the second.

The "flap" was a catcher-pitcher system based on the sign given after a total number of fingers had been thrown, with the flap being the activator. If the flap was four, the real sign came after the number of flaps added up to four, so that 1-2-1-2-1 was a curveball, as was 4-2-2-3, 3-1-2-1-2, and so forth. Sign stealers were forced to figure out the flap and whether the sign activated was the first or the second after the flap and whether it had just changed. With the flap came the "flip." With a man on second the signs might flip—change their meaning—with one gesture.[22]

7

Big Tippers

As if to prove that baseball regulated itself in 1962, over the decades since then there have been very few accusations of scoreboard spying. The most colorful occurred during the summer of 1975, when the Texas Rangers (the expansion Washington Senators) accused the Milwaukee Brewers (the former Seattle Pilots) of stationing a man in the bleachers with binoculars who passed the signals to "Bernie Brewer," a club mascot dressed in Bavarian garb and white gloves. Bernie Brewer was positioned on the outfield wall and slid down from an enormous beer keg into an enlarged beer mug every time one of the Brewers scored. The Rangers alleged that the man with the binoculars was feeding the mascot, who was signaling pitches with his white gloves. The man with the binoculars was removed from the game, and Bernie Brewer's place in the history of sign-stealing was ensured.

Since then there have been rumors but no substantial charges as to a confederate lurking in the stands stealing signs. The wildest of these came into play in 2011 when ESPN: *The Magazine* published a story that cited four anonymous players saying they saw a man in white clothing sitting in the center-field seats at the Rogers Centre in Toronto relaying signs with hand gestures. It was a fantastic story that led to the belief that a "man in white" was relaying signs to Blue Jay batters. The story eventually died for lack of evidence, and the man in white entered the realm of folklore.

Rather than relying on overt sign-stealing, managers, coaches, and players fell back on and refined their ability to interpret mannerisms and other inadvertent tip-offs. *The Sporting News* once called pitcher Bob Turley the best reader of tips in the game. Sitting in the dugout during his years with the Yankees, he was able to decipher the opposing pitcher's moves, staying silent on breaking balls and whistling to signal fastballs. Teammate Tony Kubek later extolled the worth of Turley as a code breaker: "I bet he helped Mickey Mantle hit 50 home runs over the years." Kubek also revealed that Frank Crosetti, the third base coach, became a student of Turley's system and tipped off Roger Maris before the slugger hit his sixty-first homer, breaking the record of Crosetti's old teammate Babe Ruth. "Frank saw Tracy Stallard tip the pitch, whistled, and Roger hit it out."[1]

Mantle and Maris were not the only great hitters of their time to get a little help from their more analytical teammates. "Wes Westrum was the Giants' first base coach on April 30, 1961, when Willie Mays hit four home runs in a nine-inning game," wrote columnist and baseball writer George Will. "On all four pitches that Mays hit out, Westrum—a former catcher; catchers are baseball's best empiricists—decoded the pitcher's behavior and signaled to Mays the kind of pitch that was coming." Gene Mauch has insisted that one of the reasons that Del Baker was able to stay with the Red Sox was his ability to break the pitching code and pass it along to Ted Williams.[2]

A select few pitchers seemed immune to pitch-tipping. Phillies manager Gene Mauch claimed in 1962, "Everyone has been reading Robin Roberts for 15 years and it never seemed to cramp his style; Sandy Koufax has averaged a strike out an inning since he came into the big leagues and everyone knew exactly what he was throwing. Maybe it's overrated." In 1963 Koufax lost track of the fact that just about everybody with an interest in the game knew he had two deliveries—he extended his arm in the stretch for a curve, but brought it straight down for the fastball—though this did little to help those who knew what was coming: Koufax was the National League's MVP for the year. The *New Yorker's* Roger Angell was fond of recalling a young Joe Torre catching Lew Burdette one night for the Milwaukee Braves and announcing every pitch, including a spitter, to Orlando Cepeda before it was thrown and still striking him out.[3]

Baseball officially joined the electronic age during spring training in 1968 when Minnesota, Cleveland, Washington, and several other clubs spent what was then the considerable sum of some $6,000 apiece on videotape equipment. The purpose of the new machines was to purge batters and pitchers of hitches and glitches in their swings and deliveries in large part to prevent them from tipping their tendencies.

However, the temptation to use electronics for more larcenous purposes remained, as evidenced by developments when eavesdropping equipment came into popular use. As manager of the Cubs in the late 1960s, Leo Durocher had the visiting team's clubhouse bugged. Gaylord Perry, pitching for San Francisco, later related that when the Giants detected this, they held team meetings to loudly discuss bogus pitching plans just to confuse the Cubs. In 1977 the Texas Rangers were so convinced that the Yankees were doing the same thing that they sent their own electronics expert to New York to sweep the visiting clubhouse.

The first public cry that television equipment was being used to steal signs came in June 1970 when the Royals spotted a cameraman in Robert F. Kennedy Stadium, home of the Senators in their final years in Washington. Charlie Metro, in his only year of managing the Royals, protested the offending camera and asked American League president Joe Cronin for a ruling. The Senators did not deny the camera, saying it was there to tape the game to be used the following day to analyze batters' swings.

Metro did not accept the training argument and insisted that other teams were doing it, adding, "They had one in Chicago when I was with the Cubs [on the coaching staff]. It was a closed circuit camera, and its receiver was kept in a little room behind the Cub dugout that was always locked until the game started. The picture was so clear you could see the cuticle of the catcher's fingernails." Metro, who became the Cubs manager partway into the 1962 season, then had the camera removed. "I didn't like the device and besides, our batters were so poor they couldn't hit the ball even if they knew what was coming. Once when we were using the camera against the Cards, they beat us in a doubleheader, 9–0 and 11–0."[4]

During Billy Martin's tenure as manager in Texas (1973–75), he used the club's closed-circuit television system to get signs. The next year was Martin's first managing the Yankees, and, perhaps not coincidentally, during the 1976 World Series three Yankee scouts were discovered in the press box in Cincinnati with walkie-talkies and positioned near television monitors. The Reds accused the scouts of trying to steal signs and relay them to their dugout; the Yankees said they were simply giving advice on defensive positioning. Another fifteen years passed before the National League ruled in 1991 that walkie-talkies could not be employed to align fielders from the press box. No such ruling has come from the American League.[5]

The period from the mid-1970s until the decade of the 1990s was largely devoid of accusations of stealing, with or without electronics, from any point beyond the playing field. In 1990 the first charges of theft by television in many years occurred when the Baltimore Orioles accused the Chicago White Sox of cheating by putting Coach Joe Nossek in the stands behind the first base dugout at Memorial Stadium so that he could look into the Oriole dugout, pick up signs flashed by then manager Frank Robinson, and relay them by walkie-talkie to Chicago manager Jeff Torborg. The American League dismissed the accusations. In April 1991 the Orioles again accused the White Sox of electronic espionage when they discovered that the video room at the new Comiskey Park was directly behind the White Sox dugout, providing manager Torborg and his coaches easy access to the catcher's signs, as shown by the center-field camera as well as the dugout and the third base coach. Manager Frank Robinson said, "I'm convinced they are the one team that cheats."[6]

If anything, the ethically permissible stealing by coaches and players was still a commonly practiced art. By many accounts the best decoder of signs in the business was Coach Nossek of the White Sox, formerly of the Indians and Royals, whose abilities had some calling him "the eye in the sky." For his part Nossek attributed his skill to determination, concentration, and hard work. A statistics major in college, he once told an interviewer, "My goal wasn't to become a big league ball player. It was to become a statistician for a major league club." His approach was purely analytical. "Whatever I suspected as a sign, I wrote down," he explained about learning his trade. He then spent countless hours reviewing his notes, until something fell into place and he was able to crack the code. Over time, he developed a variety of techniques to break codes, including concentrating on the moves of the opposing manager.[7]

In 1997 Nossek told *Sports Illustrated* that he might go weeks without detecting a key sign, but that when he did it could turn a game around. For instance, on April 13, 1997, Nossek stole a steal sign flashed to a man on first in the eleventh inning of a game in which the White Sox were ahead by a run. Nossek signaled his pitcher, who picked the man off. The next batter hit a home run, but instead of the Tigers being ahead by a run the game was now tied. The White Sox scored three runs in the twelfth to win the game. Indeed, some teams were said to be so afraid that their signs would be stolen by Nossek that teams came to Chicago with a new system.[8]

One change that had an impact on the number of offensive signs given—and, for that matter, stolen—in the American League came about with the advent of the designated hitter in 1973. Baseball historian Andy McCue interviewed several third base coaches in 1989. He was told by men in both leagues that there were considerably fewer signs given in the early and middle innings of American League games: by that time virtually no one was employing one-run strategies because of the DH, smaller parks in the American League, and the number of home run hitters. McCue observed, "I ran some numbers on sacrifice bunts and stolen base attempts per game and found they were considerably higher in the NL (a fan was 59% more likely to see a successful sacrifice and 34% more likely to see a stolen base attempt in an NL game in 1988). Taking an extra base is also a one-run strategy, and since an AL third base coach never has to contemplate a pitcher in the on-deck circle as a runner approaches third, he is much freer to put up the stop sign."[9]

During the 1990s sign-stealing seemed to arouse feelings of previously unexpressed personal disrespect. The tone for a new sensitivity was set when Norm Charlton of the Reds hit Mike Scioscia on the arm after realizing that Scioscia had been stealing signs from second and relaying them to the batter. Charlton claimed that what the Dodger had done was "unsportsmanlike" and admitted throwing at him: "He'll be lucky if I don't rip his head off the next time I'm pitching." Many in baseball were taken aback by this sudden and public display of anger. Gene Mauch, a Major League manager for twenty-six years, called Charlton's comments "an absolutely stupid overreaction by a guy who doesn't seem to know anything about his business and how it's transacted—or used to be, at least."[10]

In 1997 a bumper crop of accusations materialized with varying degrees of merit. The Angels claimed the Red Sox were stealing signs and to underscore the point drilled one of their batters in retaliation, while the Orioles claimed that Angels coach Larry Bowa was stepping out of the third base coaching box to steal signs flashed by Chris Hoiles, though it was later reported that the Angels were actually reading Hoiles from the dugout because he was flashing his fingers too low in his stance. Cincinnati manager Ray Knight (a former amateur boxer) nearly came to blows with Los Angeles coach Reggie Smith (a dabbler in martial arts), whom he accused of stealing catchers' signs from outside the first base coach's box.[11]

San Francisco manager Dusty Baker and Montreal manager Felipe Alou exchanged strong words over sign-stealing allegations. Baker said that Expos runners on second base were picking up the signals from the catcher and relaying them to teammates. The alleged incident took place when the Expos scored thirteen runs on thirteen hits in the sixth inning of a 19–3 victory. Baker had a point in that stealing signs in lopsided games is considered a violation of baseball's unwritten rule about running up the score when a team has a sizable lead. Alou's wry take on the squabble was to say, "At least when they accuse us of stealing signs, they're giving us credit for being intelligent, so that's good."[12]

The year 1997 also saw a season in which television again became an issue. Claims made by the Phillies that the New York Mets might be using video cameras to steal signs were looked into by the league office and disregarded. During the next visit to Shea Stadium the cable to a camera in the visitor's dugout was mysteriously cut.[13]

In May 2002 St. Louis Cardinals pitching coach Dave Duncan strongly suggested that Sammy Sosa of the Cubs had taken pitch-location signs from coaches that had allowed him to hit a lead-off home run against pitcher Matt Morris. "Somebody on their team let him know locations. We let them know we knew what they were doing and that it would be in their best interests to stop doing it," Duncan told the *St. Louis Post-Dispatch*. "Somebody might get a fastball in the ear if that's the way they want to do it," Morris said. "It's bush-league baseball. [Sosa's] an All-Star and they're tipping off location. Come on."

Sosa, a reactive hitter with a reputation for not wanting signs, was perplexed in an interview with the Associated Press: "What is amazing is that the people who don't do that, they always pick on, and the people that really do those kinds of things, they never say anything." Then Cubs manager Don Baylor called it paranoia, and the *Washington Post*'s Dave Sheinen wrote, "If the Cardinals were going to single out a player, they probably picked the wrong one in Sosa. All he has done the last four years is hit 243 homers—an average of about 61 per season."

Despite such testiness John Mizerock, bullpen coach of the Kansas City Royals, said, "The unwritten rule is that everybody is trying to steal signs." "Nothing wrong with stealing from second. That's been going on for a hundred years," said Yankee's dugout coach Don Zimmer. "It is part of the game," added Don Mattingly, then a Yankees spring training instructor. "It's your job on second base to do anything you can do to help your batter and it is the catchers' and pitchers' job not to give it away." "Picking from second is acceptable but the rule is you have to be subtle," added Rich Dauer, the Kansas City Royals' third base coach. "One thing that our guys resent is a base runner giving a body lean one way or the other on location," said Tom Gamboa, then the Royals' first base coach. "Our pitchers are working on ways to get the catcher to set up later after giving the sign because of the prevalence of sign-stealing from second base."[14]

On the other hand, many claim that one practice is universally unacceptable: a batter caught peeking back at catchers to see where the catcher is setting up or to try to pick up his signs. "In baseball, nothing is considered more verboten, or dangerous to your health, than being a sneaky peeker," writes the *Washington Post's* Tom Boswell. "The tactic is not against any written rule, but among unwritten codes, it may rank number one. . . . In this era of field-level cameras, it's doubly dangerous to fudge. Teams watch those tapes. If you're a hitter, whatever you do, don't ever get caught cutting your eyes back at the catcher at the last split second to see where he's holding his mitt as a target."[15]

To ask coaches, managers, and players if peeking is a violation of an unwritten rule is to invite terse, unequivocal answers. "That's cheating," stated St. Louis Cardinals manager Tony LaRussa in 2001, and Dallas Green, then senior adviser to the Philadelphia Phillies' general manager added, "You just can't do that." Bob Uecker has called peeking "a real no-no. Not a good idea." "If you're caught doing this," warned Dave Clark, then hitting coach for the Pittsburgh Pirates, "you're going to get hurt." To be sure, New York Mets outfielder Tsuyoshi Shinjo was caught peeking in a game against the Cardinals in 2001 and found himself on the business end of one of Matt Morris's fastballs.

By contrast, former first baseman Keith Hernandez, in his book *Pure Baseball*, put peeking into the context of baseball's morality. "Is peeking cheating? Absolutely not. Poor sportsmanship? No more than stealing signs or doctoring the ball. I consider all these tricks as part of the art and craft of playing baseball, not as cheating." On the other hand, Hernandez believes that hitting with a corked bat is cheating because there is no way of catching the trick on the field.[16]

After the 1998 season a sign-stealing controversy erupted in Japan. Sadaharu Oh, the Japanese baseball great who hit a record 868 home runs, was threatened with a lifetime ban from the game for a scheme by the team he managed, the Daiei Hawks, to steal a game. Allegedly, a team employee monitored television cameras around the Fukuoka Dome that clearly showed the opposing catcher's signals to his pitcher, then deciphered them and used a walkie-talkie to tell what pitch was coming to a confederate in the stands, who in turn relayed information to the batter via a semaphore using different positions of a megaphone. Oh was exonerated when a team investigation found no evidence of the scheme, suggesting a less than flawless policing system, but an agreement was made between the Pacific League and its clubs to punish "suspicious acts" during the course of a game, including a ban on a runner on second stealing from the catcher. In June 2001 the league slapped what the *Japan Times* called "harsh punishments," in the form of suspensions, on the general manager of the Kintetsu Buffaloes and the team scorer for violating the rule against "suspicious acts."[17]

Meanwhile, the new testiness about sign-stealing pioneered by Baker and Alou seemed to be more common, and, real or imagined, stealing from second was becoming serious business, likely to get somebody hurt. On May 3, 2002, Tampa Bay put out the word that Nomar Garciaparra was stealing signs from second base, helping Shea Hillenbrand to hit a grand slam, an idea Garciaparra and Hillenbrand ridiculed. But Tampa's Ryan Rupe threw at Nomar and hit Hillenbrand in retaliation.

"Signs are more important today than ever before," said Ed Ott in 2001 when he was the bullpen coach for the Detroit Tigers, and there are more signals today than when he came up in 1974 with the Pirates. "These days you have to be a graduate of MIT to get all the signals." Taught and drilled at every level of the game above Little League through Triple A, today's Major

League rookies are fluent in the art of nonverbal communication by the time they come up, and stories of players who cannot keep it all straight are few and far between. Teams work hard to keep their signals straight and strong and as "steal-proof" as possible, especially when it comes to the battery. "We have three different sets of signs," said Elrod Hendricks, Baltimore Orioles bullpen coach in 2001. "We can switch from one to another at any given moment. Middle infielders have to know what is going on. We can change our system two or three times in an inning if we have to."[18]

Billy Hatcher, third base coach for the Tampa Bay Devil Rays in 2001, says that signs are of such importance that he reviews them with his players at least once a week. "Any time a sign is missed; it's going to cost you a ball game, so you gotta make sure they are ready." As part of that 2001 conversation Jerry Narron, then third base coach and manager for the Texas Rangers, said, "Even in this day of players who are paid in the millions, there is a cost for missing a sign." "They make sure they know signs in this organization," says Mickey Rivers, a Yankees spring training instructor. "They make sure everyone understands, and if you miss one we will fine you."

Despite the constant use of video equipment and the sharp eyes of instructors and coaches to spot telltale habits, recent history suggests that a significant number of pitchers still tip their pitches—a reminder of how hard it is for anyone to perform an act exactly the same way every time. The tip-offs have ranged from the Pirates' Joe Beimel flaring his glove on off-speed pitches to the placement of Hideki Irabu's feet, which gave Peter Gammons the line "Now teams hit him well because, though Irabu speaks no English, he can be read."[19]

Two of baseball's most celebrated incidents of pitch tip-offs have come in the postseasons of 2001 and 2002. In Game Six of the 2001 World Series, Yankees left-hander Andy Pettitte was given the ball for the possible clincher against the Arizona Diamondbacks, only to be driven from the mound early in a 15–2 drubbing. "He wasn't just tipping his pitches," wrote *Sport's Illustrated*'s Tom Verducci. "He practically grabbed the PA microphone and announced them." Rick Sutcliffe, the former Cy Young winner, noted during the international telecast of the game that Pettitte was tipping and, to make the point, proceeded to correctly predict forthcoming pitches.

The telltale signs came when Pettitte was pitching out of the stretch. If he brought his hands to his belt in an arc he would deliver a curveball, while after lowering his hands in a direct line he threw a fastball. The Arizona hitters picked up on the pattern almost immediately, evening up the Series and winning it all the next night.

In a postgame interview Yankee skipper Joe Torre admitted "the possibility" that Arizona hitters might have known what Pettitte was going to throw, based on "the fact that they sometimes ignored tough pitches on the fringe of the strike zone, and Pettitte's own history of tipping pitches." Later, after reviewing game tapes, Torre confirmed that it had happened. In the heat of the moment he and his talented staff had missed Pettitte's faux pas.

In 2002 the Diamondbacks were on the giving end. This time it came up on the eve of the 2001 divisional playoffs. In two late-season starts—September 25 against the Cardinals and September 29 against the Rockies—Curt Schilling tipped his pitches to the degree that Sutcliffe, again in the broadcast booth, was able to predict sixteen straight pitches during the September 29 telecast. This no doubt explained Schilling's poor September, during which his ERA was 5.87 and he allowed seventeen hits in his final sixteen and a third innings. Sutcliffe spoke with Schilling after the game and helped him iron out his problem before his first start in the playoffs. He was his usual overpowering self during the Diamondbacks' 2–1 loss in his first start of the playoffs.

Ironically, Schilling's tipping problem seemed to pass to team-mate Randy Johnson, the unanimous choice for the National League Cy Young Award in 2002. He gave up six runs in a 12–2 pasting in the first divisional playoff game against the Cardinals, and Sutcliffe suggested that he had been tipping his pitches with his hands. Johnson admitted the possibility: "It's not the first time I've heard that I was tipping my pitches. I've pitched against [Tony] LaRussa and his coaching staff enough times that if there was any kind of flaw I'm sure they would be the first to see that."

8

Epitaph for a Miracle

In a front-page story during the January off-season of 2001—the fiftieth anniversary year of the Miracle of Coogan's Bluff—the *Wall Street Journal* brought the most famous stolen sign and sign-stealing scheme in baseball history back to life.

The original allegations brought up during spring training in 1962 seemed largely forgotten by the time that regular season started. The stars of the final moment in the "miracle," Bobby Thomson and Ralph Branca, had continued to talk about their historic encounter as friends and without any public comment on the anonymous allegation that Thomson had gotten the sign for Branca's pitch. In February 1952 the two debuted their hero-and-goat act in an appearance on *The Ed Sullivan Show*. The dour Sullivan introduced the two with an explanation that they were about to perform a parody written by sportswriter Jack Mann for that winter's annual Baseball Writers Association of America dinner. Thomson walked onto the stage in his New York Giants uniform and, pointing to a large hanging photo of Branca, began to sing, *Because of you, there's a song in my heart*... When Thomson was done, Branca appeared onstage in his Dodgers garb, pointed to an oversize photo of Thomson, and then began to sing, *Because of you, I should have never been born*...[1] Thirty years later a headline for a 1982 story on the endless round of banquet-circuit appearances being made by Branca and Thomson exclaimed THOMSON HOMER WEARS WELL.[2]

That the Giants were stealing signs with a buzzer system in 1951 was undeniable. However, whenever the buzzer story was revived, Thomson denied that he had benefited from it in any way. For a 1968 issue of the *American Legion Magazine* he was asked if he had been tipped for that fastball: "No, I never wanted to know what pitch was coming. I was so over eager, if I'd known a fastball was coming I'd likely have swung too soon and missed it."[3] Joseph Reichler, who had written the original 1962 story, died in 1988. He had received the J. G. Taylor Spink Award for his lifetime contribution to baseball writing and edited several editions of *The Baseball Encyclopedia*. He spent the last nineteen years of his life before retirement working for the commissioner and Major League Productions. In his later years Reichler wrote about the Thomson home run in detail on several occasions, never again alluding to the sign-stealing operation and never hinting that Thomson had been tipped off.[4]

For his part, in 1991 Thomson celebrated the fortieth anniversary of his feat in a book titled *The Giants Win the Pennant! The Giants Win the Pennant!* in which Thomson and his two cowriters reported, "Stealing signs, or trying to steal signs, has always been a big part of baseball. Everybody does it. Some of the methods are crude, others ingenious." He then openly discussed the fact that Durocher had such an operation in place in 1951 and gave eyewitness reports on how both the Giants and the Dodgers got away with it during the period.[5]

The *Wall Street Journal* article, by Joshua Harris Prager, revived what had been for the most part a dormant story. It asserted what everyone admitted, that the Giants had been using an elaborate system to steal opponents' signs during the season and in the playoffs against the Dodgers. Outfielder Monte Irvin, catcher Sal Yvars, and pitcher Al Gettel acknowledged the sign-stealing scheme, just as many Giants had not denied the fact in 1962, though they denied that Thomson took the sign on his famous homer. In the *Journal* article, however, bullpen catcher Yvars maintained that he had given Thomson the sign from his position in the outfield bullpen, an admission he had made for many years on the banquet circuit.

Prager's research suggested that the Giants got to be in a position for Thomson to hit the "Shot Heard 'Round the World" with the use of a telescope (not binoculars, as was reported in 1962) in the clubhouse situated in center field at the Polo Grounds, by which the catcher's signs were stolen and relayed via an electric buzzer to the bullpen in left center field and from there to the batter.

Thomson again denied that he had taken the sign on the famous pitch. "My answer is no," he was quoted as saying. But he also indicated he felt some guilt over the scheme, which he did not deny. "I guess I've been a jerk in a way," he said. "That I don't want to face the music. Maybe I've felt too sensitive, embarrassed maybe."[6]

The response to Prager's piece was enormous and without precedent for a modern baseball story. In the hundreds of follow-up articles and columns was a mixture of opinion. Some were ready to punish: "If Pete Rose can be kept out of Cooperstown, perhaps Durocher should be removed," wrote Tom Boswell in the *Washington Post*. "His greatest feat, by far, was the '51 comeback. Could his Giants have come from 13 1/2 games behind in mid-August without cheating?"[7] Others felt that Branca could now stop playing the role of victim. "After nearly 50 years as one of the greatest scapegoats in sports, Ralph Branca finally is feeling a measure of redemption," David Waldstein wrote in the *Newark (NJ) Star-Ledger*.[8] Some took Thomson at his word and declared that everyone in that era was trying to steal signs and that it was not a story.[9] Others, including a few Dodgers, were more amused than angry. "It doesn't surprise me. Leo Durocher would do almost anything to win a ball game," said Hall of Fame outfielder Duke Snider to the *New York Post*, "but it doesn't change anything. Everyone *steals* signs. It's part of the game. We were stealing signs," he said. Still he was asked whether the Dodgers were using a spyglass in the clubhouse and a buzzer to the bullpen and dugout. "No," Snider added, then admitted, "But that's because we never thought of it."[10]

The Dodger catcher that day was Rube Walker, who had replaced the injured Roy Campanella. When interviewed in the mid-1970s by Thomas Kiernan for his book *The Miracle of Coogan's Bluff*, Walker stated his "steal-proof system" that year consisted of seven different finger-and-fist configurations flashed in sequence, that the "active" sign for the desired pitch was just one of the seven in the sequence, and that the active sign's number in the sequence was changed every few innings.[11] Whitey Lockman, the Giant runner on second with Thomson at the plate, has long maintained that he couldn't read Walker's signs. "I didn't recognize the sequence," Lockman, now seventy-four, told the *Wall Street Journal*, adding that he touched his belt buckle to let Thomson know he couldn't read the sign. This is essentially what Lockman said in 1962, when the story first broke, and it seems again to support Thomson's assertion that he didn't get the sign. If Lockman could not decode the sign from second, it is also hard to imagine that someone in the outfield, even with a telescope, could have recognized the new sequence of signs and buzzed in the result to be relayed to Thomson in time.

"Since the story broke a number of observers have pointed out that New York's remarkable turnaround in the second half of the season, when they finished 51-18, came about because of improved pitching," wrote Glenn Stout in his 2002 book, *Yankees Century: One Hundred Years of New York Yankee Baseball*.[12] The leading advocate of this is David W. Smith of Retrosheet, a group attempting to collect and disseminate play-by-play accounts of every Major League game in history. Smith researched the Giants' record for the entire season and found that although

New York went 51-18 after they began stealing signs (including 24-6 at the Polo Grounds), the Giants actually hit worse at home after that point than before. On the morning of July 20—the day the scheme went into effect—the Giants were batting .263 at home and .252 on the road. For the rest of the season New York hit .256 in the Polo Grounds and .269 away. Conversely, before July 20 the Giants' pitching staff had a 3.44 ERA at home and 4.53 on the road; after July 20 their ERA was 2.80 at home and 3.00 away.[13] "So, did the sign-stealing occur?" Smith asked himself in an unpublished July 2002 paper titled "Play by Play Analysis of the 1951 National League Pennant Race." "Probably. Did it help? Apparently not. Of course, it only has to be true that the sign-stealing helped them win one more game than they would have lost in order to end up the season in a tie. My point is simple: There is no evidence in the data that sign-stealing was a significant factor in the great comeback of the 1951 Giants. Remember that the Giants' record did not begin its dramatic improvement until August 12."[14]

Little discussed in the debate that came in the wake of the *Wall Street Journal* revelations was that the story had been in circulation for many years. Prager regarded them as inconsequential when he wrote, "Indeed, a few times over 50 years, rumors that the 1951 Giants stole signs circulated in the press and sports literature. But they came to nothing. . . . The secret was safe." The notable exception was Howard Kleinbcrg, a former editor of the *Miami News* and now a columnist for the Cox News Service, who had a sense of déjà vu and recalled that he had a copy of Thomson's 1991 book, in which he found that Thomson openly discussed the scheme. It included quotes from Dick Williams, who was with the Dodgers and said, "Leo definitely had a guy in the clubhouse stealing signs with a spyglass. He'd beep it to one of their guys in the bull pen, who would then relay it in." Kleinberg wrote in his column for February 18, 2001, in the *Chattanooga Times*, "This makes the *Wall Street*

Journal story old news to me and raises a question as to why it was resurrected as we approach the 50th anniversary of the event if for any reason other than to expunge the moment from its place in history."[15]

One small but salient point in the *Wall Street Journal* piece was this assertion, reprinted by virtually everyone writing about the incident in the wake of the story: "It wasn't until 1961 that Major League Baseball passed a rule banning sign-stealing by way of a 'mechanical device.'" Yet there is no evidence that such a ban was ever put into place. In the intervening half century many writers have asserted that there is no rule against stealing of any kind. For instance, in Leonard Koppett's *The New Thinking Man's Guide to Baseball*, considered among the best primers on the game ever written, he brings up the issue of agents with binoculars in center field or in scoreboards and then asserts: "There has never been a specific rule against this, but it is generally considered unethical, because the home team can arrange it while the visiting team cannot." Other than the comments by Warren Giles and Ford Frick—that if such a transgression was "proven," and if it led to a win, the transgressing team would forfeit that game—there is absolutely nothing else in the record.[16]

In July 2001 Home Box Office aired a documentary to celebrate the fiftieth anniversary of the famous game. Thomson again denied getting the sign during the three-day series, although he admitted taking them in the regular season. Thomson's teammates Monte Irvin and Al Corwin agreed. Corwin said that even when the system worked, it was cumbersome and sometimes "less than accurate."[17]

Did Thomson rely on a stolen sign for his famous home run? There is not a scintilla of hard evidence to show that he did. The only "proof" comes from an anonymous player who did not join the Giants until two years after the event and from the latter-day testimony of Sal Yvars, who claims he could tell that Thomson had actually taken a signal from five hundred feet away. Thus, there is no reason not to take Thomson at his word.

Whatever could be said of the behavior of the 1951 Giants, including Thomson in the days leading up to the playoffs, it could not be labeled anything worse than unethical, which is exactly what Christy Mathewson had called the use of spyglasses decades earlier and what most baseball people would call it today. The line crossed by the 1951 Giants was, for its time, the norm and still is after all these years perfectly legal.

In 2006 Joshua Prager published *The Echoing Green: The Untold Story of Bobby Thomson, Ralph Branca and the Shot Heard Round the World*, a highly regarded book that focused more on the era and the remarkable relationship between Ralph Branca and Bobby Thomson. In a concluding author's note he added, "And I say that as regards the stealing of signs, my book is not about the debatable effects of a telescope on play but about the undeniable effects of a secret on two men."[18]

9

Devious Digital Devices—from the
TV Camera to the Apple Watch

In 1965, just after he had left his position as a coach for the Los Angeles Dodgers, the once eternally controversial Leo Durocher signed on as a television commentator for the ABC *Game of the Week*. As both a player and a manager, Durocher was known for his ability to mouth off, earning him the nickname "the Lip." The American Broadcasting Company was banking on Leo to say and do outrageous things to boost ratings on the show. They were hardly disappointed.

On May 8 Vice President Hubert Humphrey went to the ballpark to see the Washington Senators play. This was also Durocher's first game as an ABC commentator in Washington, and Humphrey was invited to join Leo in the broadcast booth. Durocher decided that this would be the perfect moment to start stealing signs and calling pitches before they were thrown. With the aid of cameras placed by ABC in the dugout and outfield, Leo gave the vice president a quick lesson in how to pick up signs and decode them. Humphrey was clearly nervous about being put in this position as an accomplice and observed flatly that there were no secrets anymore. Durocher and ABC were rebuked by the commissioner's office for both the cameras and the live larceny.[1]

This was certainly not the first example of electronic espionage in baseball, but it was the first to generate interest beyond the sports pages. The ever-controversial Durocher had not only willfully gotten himself into a jam but also used the vice president of the United States as his foil.

In the decades that followed a few other examples of electronic espionage came to light, most of which have been discussed earlier. The powers that be paid only minimal attention, and charges against teams for the use of walkie-talkies and television equipment were often dismissed with a shrug of the shoulder and a fine by league officials, who still held major power over disciplining teams in their separate leagues.

However, a major change went into effect in September 1999, as power in the system shifted from the two leagues and their powerful presidents to the commissioner and the entity known to this day as Major League Baseball. "This is an historic moment that many have felt was long overdue," said Commissioner Bud Selig, who spearheaded the move to consolidate such matters as umpiring, scheduling, and discipline. At the same time, Selig stressed that the leagues would remain separate and competitive on the field. Between this and a new empowering constitution that was created in the wake of the consolidation, Selig now had more power than even the first commissioner, Kenisaw Mountain Landis, who referred to himself as "high commissioner" and was given the title of "czar" by the press.[2]

The shift in power was accomplished at a time when much of humankind had become fearful of a digital apocalypse caused by the mysterious "Y2K bug," which, depending on whom you listened to, would render household appliances and ATMs inoperable; some agonized over nuclear power plants shutting down, planes crashing, and the triggering of an unintended nuclear war. It all came to naught; the panic subsided before dawn on January 1, 2000. The billions spent by government and private companies to prepare seemed like a total waste. If there was an aftereffect other than having given a spur to the nascent survivalist movement, it was that we had become dependent on all things digital and somehow lost something in the process.

This lesson was not lost on Major League Baseball, because early in 2000 MLB operations chief Sandy Alderson effectively laid down the law with a memo distributed to all teams: "Please be reminded that the use of electronic equipment during a game is restricted. No club shall use electronic equipment, including walkie-talkies and cellular telephones, to communicate to or with any on-field personnel, including those in the dugout, bullpen, and field and—during the game—the clubhouse. Such equipment may not be used for the purpose of stealing signs or conveying information designed to give a club an advantage."

In the wake of this ban, smartphones, laptops, and any device that connected with the Internet were banned from the field, the dugout, and the bullpen. If a coach or member of the staff wanted to use a laptop in the dugout, it could only be one provided by MLB, which featured the inability to use the Internet.

Slowly—very slowly—things changed.

In January 2013 MLB engaged in a new multiyear, multimillion-dollar partnership with T-Mobile, announced at the Consumer Electronics Show in Las Vegas, that would equip managers and their pitching coaches with special phones that would communicate only between the two. The deal was to establish a special T-Mobile network inside each stadium using "geofencing" (a fancy word for blocking) to keep the phones from operating outside the dugout and bullpen and keeping the Internet turned off at the ballpark. The ancient landlines between the dugout and bullpen would be replaced with a Samsung Galaxy S3 digital equivalent in the 2014 season.[3]

As if to mark the final days of the old-fashioned phones at the ballpark, while David Ortiz of the Boston Red Sox was playing the Baltimore Orioles later in the 2013 season, he struck out in the seventh inning, got really upset, got ejected, and then shattered a dugout phone with a few monster swings of the bat.[4] Although the phone casing lay in pieces on the dugout floor, the phone still worked.[5]

But along came 2014, and the T-Mobile deal somehow became undone, so baseball and the teams of the MLB reverted to the old, sometimes reliable station-to-station landlines. The new digital era never dawned, and the telephonic technology that was state of the art in the time of the 1929 stock-market crash was back in business.

All that was digital was not lost. With the start of the 2014 season, all teams were given access to video-replay technology, which provided several flat-screen monitors with up to fourteen camera angles. Each team has a staff member monitoring games on the equipment in case there is a ruling the team wants to appeal, but it is also common for players to mill about and watch the game on those screens.

As more cameras and monitoring devices showed up on the field, it became increasingly common and then the norm for pitchers and catchers to cover their mouths with their gloves when they met on the mound to foil lip-readers studying high-definition images.

In June 2014 Houston Astros general manager Jeff Luhnow told reporters the team had been the victim of hackers, who accessed servers and proceeded to publish months of internal trade talks. This was the beginning of a cybernetic scandal of unprecedented proportion, as the St. Louis Cardinals were accused of hacking into the computers of the Astros and accessing their scouting reports.

This was suddenly not an "inside baseball" event but a real felony in which federal laws had been broken. The Cardinals' scouting director, Chris Correa, was charged. His legal defense was that he hacked the Cardinals based on his suspicion that the Astros had misappropriated proprietary material from the Cardinals.

The judge hearing the case listened to Correa's explanation, looked at the defendant, and asked, "So you broke in their house to find out if they were stealing your stuff?" Correa replied, "Stupid, I know."

The evidence compiled by the Federal Bureau of Investigation showed that Correa's theft had begun in 2013, when he improperly gained access to a file of the Astros' scouting list of every eligible player for that year's draft. The prosecutor said that he had improperly viewed notes of trade discussions as well as a page that listed information such as potential bonus details, statistics, and notes on recent performances and injuries by team prospects.[6]

Correa was sentenced in July 2016 to forty-six months in federal prison and ordered to pay $279,038 in restitution after pleading guilty to five counts of intrusion. Then baseball stepped in and imposed a $2 million fine on the Cardinals and their two top picks in the upcoming 2017 amateur draft, which ended up being the fifty-sixth and seventy-fifth picks overall.

The punishment meted out by the commissioner was not something routine or traditional (such as depriving the team of a previous title, which is a practice of the National Collegiate Athletic Association, or removing a medal, in a case involving the Olympics) but geared to the future, where it could have a long-term impact. If the draft is the lifeblood of a successful franchise, the Cardinals had lost a key piece of their future, and the Astros, who would go on to win the 2017 World Series championship, had gained significantly not just for the present but almost certainly for the future.

Baseball's amateur draft had become increasingly important since it was created in 1965 and was seen as the quickest path to acquiring top prospects at a reasonable price. For that reason much of both the new emphasis on analytics and the traditional reliance on a network of scouts is aimed at whom a team will pick in the draft. The success of the Astros in

2017 was in large part the result of canny draft picks during the three consecutive seasons in which they lost more than 100 games (2011, 106 losses; 2012, 107 losses; 2013, 111 losses) and could work with high draft positions. So now that the commissioner showed that he was able to impose fines but also to reassign draft picks, the power of the office was significantly enhanced.

At the beginning of the 2017 season, all teams got a new version of the 2000 directive that now banned any handheld electronic device. "The only exceptions to this prohibition are the use of a mobile phone for communication between the dugout and the bullpen, and the use of tablets in the dugout or bullpen running uniform programs, so long as such devices and programs have been approved by the Office of the Commissioner."

In August 2017 New York Yankees general manager Brian Cashman filed a detailed complaint with the commissioner's office that included a video the Yankees shot of the Red Sox dugout during a three-game series between the two teams earlier in the month. Cashman alleged that a member of the Red Sox training staff was getting information on his Apple Watch from the Fenway Park video room, decoding signs being flashed by the Yankee catcher that would be passed along to the trainer, who then relayed the information to other players in the dugout. They, in turn, would signal the man at bat about the type of pitch that was about to be thrown.[7]

Apple Watches of the kind allegedly abused by the Red Sox were permitted as of 2015, but only as timepieces rather than as communications devices—essentially a Timex that needed to be recharged and carried a monthly fee to a provider.

Baseball investigators corroborated the Yankees' claims based on video the commissioner's office uses for instant replay and broadcasts. The commissioner's office then confronted the Red Sox, who admitted that their trainers had received signals from video-replay personnel and then relayed that information to

Red Sox players—an operation that had been in place for at least several weeks.

The fine was $500,000. The Red Sox, which had responded to the initial charge by accusing the Yankees of using a YES Network camera to steal signs, a charge that MLB did not act on as it swept the episode away. Although Commissioner Rob Manfred, in his statement, said baseball's investigators had found "insufficient evidence" to support Boston's counterclaim that the Yankees had used a YES Network camera to inappropriately steal signs from the Red Sox, New York was fined a lesser, undisclosed, amount for a transgression from a previous championship season when they violated the rules governing the use of a dugout phone. Those who read this decision and knew anything about baseball's history were perplexed, to say the least. What "previous championship season" did the edict refer to—2009 or any one of another eleven going back to 1949 and earlier?

When the announcement was made that a fine would be imposed, Manfred said, "Taking all of these factors as well as past precedent into account, I have decided to fine the Red Sox an undisclosed amount which in turn will be donated by my office to hurricane relief efforts in Florida. Moreover, all 30 Clubs have been notified that future violations of this type will be subject to more serious sanctions, including the possible loss of draft picks."[8]

The Red Sox did suffer the indignity of seeming foolish not only in getting caught but also in making such an obvious and illegal move. "Boston's real transgression here wasn't stealing signs," wrote Steven Goldman on *Slate*. "It was using technology where none was needed. Strapping on an Apple Watch was neither devious nor clever. It served only to make the scheme more obvious, and thus ultimately useless." Jim Souhan of the *Minneapolis Star-Tribune* looked at the transgression and wrote, "The Red Sox were more stupid than evil. Using television cameras and a high-tech watch probably didn't help them markedly more than old-fashioned sign stealing would have. The Sox jeopardized the franchise's reputation and risked penalty trying to be clever, when truly clever players have been stealing signs effectively for a century or more."[9] Or as Bob Nightengale put it in USA *Today*, "Steal signs? Sure. Just use your eyes, and not your i-s"—that is, *i* as in "iPhone."[10]

On February 19, 2018, MLB announced that it was in the process of installing new dedicated landline telephone lines between dugouts and video rooms that would be monitored and recorded by MLB as a means of deterring sign-stealing by those on the field. Susan Jacoby, author of *Why Baseball Matters*, commented in *Time* in May 2018, "New phone lines connect each club's video-review rooms and the dugout, with the supposed purpose of monitoring communications and discouraging sign-stealing. I must confess that I have always found sign-stealing an amusing part of the game—one which any team whose manager has a brain can find other ways to discourage."

On the same day, MLB announced that beginning with the regular season, mound visits would be restricted to six during a nine-inning game, with an additional visit for each extra inning in a tie game. Visits by a manager to change pitchers do not count, and umpires can award additional visits by the catcher if his signals with the pitcher get crossed up. Those will be granted on the request of the catcher on a case-by-case basis.

Most teams immediately added the initials MVR (for "mound visits remaining") on their stadium scoreboards as an additional column in the line score. Pencil-and-paper scorecard keepers now got to use a new hieroglyphic to note the exact moment when each mound visit took place.

The reason for the decision was part of the "pace of play" reforms being pursued by Commissioner Rob Manfred, intended to speed up the game. As Eduardo A. Encina explained in the *Baltimore Sun*, "Limiting the number of mound visits to six was a compromise from the league office to the players union, which opposed MLB's plan to establish a pitch clock that included game-altering penalties." The mound-visit rule was imposed unilaterally by Manfred, who saw it as a way to cut the time of an average game from three hours and five minutes, which had been achieved in 2017, up an average of about fourteen minutes from 2010.

Visits to the mound by catchers had become increasingly frequent in recent seasons, especially in the late innings of crucial games and when the opposing team had a runner on second base. As Justin Verlander told Tyler Kepner of the *New York Times* on the day the rule change was announced, pitchers and catchers were meeting more often now to combat sign-stealing, which has become much more sophisticated with advanced video technology. "The signs are getting so much more advanced to protect against that, so that's why you're seeing more mound visits," Verlander said. "And when guys get on base, the game comes to a screeching halt. I don't think the adjustments they made here are going to change anything. A few minutes, maybe."

But Dave Martinez, the manager of the Washington Nationals, was not sure six visits would be enough. "It's hard to say, it really is," Martinez said. "We had a pitcher-catcher relationship day today, and we brought that up. The biggest thing is not getting anybody hurt. That's our concern. Especially umpires, if there's any miscommunication with signs."[11]

The dilemma all of this posed was also backed up by the increasing belief that there is something immoral about sign-stealing and that it is not an inherent part of the game itself. Not long ago a Michigan newspaper asked various religious leaders the question of whether the practice was immoral, and one minister said that it was but only if it showed malicious intent.[12]

Even before the Apple Watch–gate incident, Commissioner Manfred said that he had had complaints from players about sign-stealing and how it impacted the pace of play with men on base. He described sign-stealing as "a form of behavior that we should not tolerate"—an opinion that was shared by few in the game, who see espionage on the field as integral to the sport.[13]

The fact of the matter is that the lore and history of baseball are so intertwined with signs and sign-stealing that it would seem all but impossible to stop it. It is one thing to spot a set of binoculars or an Apple Watch being studied rather than used as a timepiece, but it is something else entirely to rein in those who do so through concentration and brainpower. A case in point came when MLB announced it would rewire all the ballparks, and Cubs manager Joe Maddon said that he was not concerned with the new monitored phone lines but then boasted about his past life as a sign stealer. "I used to be really good at picking up signs from the other team," said Maddon, who served as a coach with the Angels from 1994 to 2005. "I'm not any more. When you're not managing, you have this real ability to put your focus somewhere else more readily. Whereas when you're managing, you have specific things you're focused on all the time."

Maddon went on to call sign-stealing an art that he had learned from former Cubs manager Preston Gomez, who served as a third base coach and former executive in the Angels organization." He added, "But you got to pay attention to every sign given," which includes looking for an indicator that a sign is live.[14]

Days after the Red Sox's tap on the wrist, baseball was treated to an extraordinary and possibly unprecedented moment when a fan with a good view of the catcher and a strong set of lungs bellowed out information to the Yankees' Gary Sanchez while he was hitting in the eighth inning of his team's game with the Tampa Bay Rays. Sanchez heard the voice, but so did Rays catcher Wilson Ramos and the home-plate umpire, Dan Bellino, who pointed out the man to stadium security and had him removed from the stadium. The fan has not been identified. "You could definitely hear the guy screaming, 'Outside, outside,' but you don't know if it's going to be a slider or a fastball," Sanchez said afterward. "You got to stick to your plan, whatever plan you have, regardless of what people are screaming."

Ramos confirmed that the fan's observations were accurate. "That was not professional," he told the Associated Press after Tuesday's game. "If you come to the game, you're asked to enjoy the game. Everybody's supposed to see the ball and just react with pitches . . . so to me, it's like cheating."

After the fan was ejected, Sanchez hit a bloop single to drive in the Yankees' fifth run in a game that the men from the Bronx won 6–1 over the Tampa Bay Rays. After the game Yankees manager Joe Girardi was asked what he heard and said, "Someone in the stands was yelling out location for one or two pitches while Gary was up. I heard it for one or two pitches. Rightfully so, they were removed from the park. That shouldn't happen." But it did happen. The fan was ejected for sign-stealing, perhaps the first such ejection in the history of the game.[15]

Another interesting development early in 2018 had nothing to do with electronics but involved the simple and legal tactic of a second baseman standing in front of the base runner at second in an effort to shield him from view of the catcher's signs, an old-school wrinkle introduced by Cubs shortstop Javier Báez in April.

It would appear, at least at this writing near the end of the 2018 season, that the specter of electronic sign-stealing has not raised its head. I asked Barry Svrluga, national sportswriter for the *Washington Post*, for his take on the state of sign-stealing in 2018, and he replied, "I would say, loosely, that old-school sign-stealing certainly goes on, that teams consider it their responsibility to guard against it, and that I'd be surprised if there was a lot of electronic sign-stealing happening because MLB has said it would come down hard on people."[16]

If anything, what seemed to be working best in the world of baseball espionage in 2017–18 were the old-school techniques that had nothing to do with electronic devices. Watching for pitchers to tip their pitches was still a major factor. The success of the Houston Astros in their rise from the cellar to a world championship in 2017 had many fathers, but one was the leadership role of Carlos Beltrán, the veteran outfielder signed by the Astros after the 2016 season who brought with him an uncanny singular ability to study opposing pitchers and determine their "tells"—gestures and small changes in behavior that signaled whether the next pitch would be, for example, a breaking ball or a fastball. According to Ben Reiter in *Astroball: The New Way to Win It All*, a remarkable account of how Houston went from worst to best, Beltrán not only interpreted opposing pitchers but also corrected "tells" for the pitchers who were his teammates. On first meeting pitcher Dallas Keuchel at spring training in 2017, Beltrán noted the pitcher's rising ERA in the 2016 season and said, "Sometimes you held your hand above the ball last year before a pitch. If the ball showed it was a fastball. If it didn't it was an off-speed pitch." According to Reiter, Keuchel said he appreciated the information and went on to have a much-improved 2017 season.[17] The practice of a base runner on second base stealing signs—or at least attempting to—was as commonly practiced in 2018 as it had been for decades.

At another level the aforementioned allegation that the Toronto Blue Jays had a "man in white" stealing signs was still being voiced around the Majors during the 2018 season. The myth is an urban legend, pure and simple, that has been talked about for more than a decade, yet there's no shred of concrete evidence that sign-stealing from the stands by a man in white was taking place at the Rogers Centre. The rumor was given major impetus in 2011 when ESPN: *The Magazine* reported that several pitchers had anonymously reported a man in white who raised his hands for slower breaking pitches and did nothing for fastballs. In the intervening years Toronto fans have gleefully fed the rumor by dressing in white and feeding the myth.[18]

Throughout the 2018 season a deep awareness of sign-stealing prevailed, and elaborate schemes were put into play to thwart it. During the American League Championship Series (ALCS) playoffs, Houston Astros manager A. J. Hitch told Tyler Kepner of the *New York Times*, "We ask a lot of our catchers. We have 12, 13, sometimes 14 pitchers on a roster that can all have different signs and different sequences." The team also changed signs even when there were no men on base, assuming some level of espionage was taking place in the stands. The Astros also employed members of the team's travel party to roam the ballparks of other teams to make sure sign-stealing was not going on.[19]

Hitch revealed all of this to Kepner after an incident during the first game of the ALCS playoffs between the Boston Red Sox and the Astros at Fenway Park when a member of the Astros staff was discovered by Major League Baseball security in a restricted area near the Red Sox dugout. The immediate question was whether the man in question was involved in stealing signs.

The story was kept quiet until the third game, when a statement was put out by Major League Baseball that confirmed that the incident had occurred but had determined that the Astros employee in question was only trying to see into Boston's dugout to make sure the Red Sox weren't stealing Astros signs, as opposed to stealing Red Sox signs himself. The terse statement ended with the statement, "We consider the matter closed."[20]

The story was anything but closed to the rest of the baseball world and dominated the nation's sports pages and sports radio call-in shows for the next twenty-four-hour cycle and provided a host of thoughts and opinions, including by some who felt something more insidious was at play and that MLB had been too quick to declare the Astro agent innocent, especially without a more detailed explanation. One commentator pointedly asked, "Major League Baseball expects you to believe the kid wasn't cheating? He snuck into a forbidden area to tape illegally and make sure the Red Sox weren't cheating?"[21]

Buster Olney of ESPN tweeted prior to the fourth game, "Many team officials across baseball frustrated, appalled by MLB decision on Astros/spygate. They believe that Rob Manfred threatened in past to come down hard on violators of electronic surveillance rule, and now with crystal-clear evidence of HOU breaking rules, nothing happens."

Suddenly, on September 18, word came that the Milwaukee Brewers were openly suggesting the Los Angeles Dodgers were using video to electronically steal signs from them during the National League Championship Series. Some saw the incident as a reflection of a larger fear permeating the game that now bordered on paranoia. One of these was David Sheinin of the *Washington Post*, who wrote that it was commonly assumed that an essential system that makes the game function properly was broken. "No," he wrote, "baseball doesn't have a sign-stealing problem. It has a technology problem." He commented on the ratcheting up of paranoia throughout the game, which had become common during the 2018 season. "No longer is it just the runner on second base with a clear view of the catcher's hands that teams have to worry about and have to change their signs to thwart. Now it's that guy in the center-field seats with the telescoping camera or the strength coach in the dugout with the smart watch or the dude in the camera well with a tablet."[22]

This paranoia, like any other weakness in baseball, can also be exploited by consciously or unconsciously giving the appearance that one might be engaging in espionage. After the Red Sox won the 2018 ALCS, Boston manager Alex Cora appeared on a Boston radio show and said that he wasn't angry with the Astros. On the contrary, he indicated his happiness at the apparent effect it had on his opposition: "I took it the other way around because they openly said that they were playing defense. They said they were checking on us if we were stealing signs, or doing something wrong in the dugout. . . . Paranoia is working for us. . . . They are panicking. Throughout the series, we did a lot of stuff as far as like dummy signs and all this stuff to keep the paranoia going."

As far as sign-stealing, Cora noted in his WEEI interview that he saw nothing wrong with it: "That is part of the game—tipping, stealing signs, relaying pitches and paying attention to details. That is the way I took it. If they feel that way about us, we might as well push the envelope and keep doing a lot of things that are going to make them uncomfortable and you saw it. They kept changing signs and the tempo of the games was awful, but that worked into our advantage."[23]

The digital paranoia that infected the Majors did not seem to spread to other levels of the game, where the old-school approach still seemed to be in play. Mario Porto, the head baseball coach at Moorpark College in Moorpark, California, who was coaching for the Big Train, a summer collegiate baseball team in Bethesda, Maryland, in a July 2018 dugout discussion of the state of the art of signs said, "Youngsters are now learning the art of giving, taking, and stealing signs in youth baseball, and by the time they are playing college ball they can adapt to any system of signing." Porto added that college players are keenly aware of "tells," and many are expert at quickly detecting them. When asked about his own system of signing, he said he uses a series of set signs for batters and base runners that are the same but can be given from three different levels: the head, the waist, or the lower body. So when he says, "Hats are hot tonight," that means the real signs are gestures made with the head.[24]

Conclusion

How to Really Watch a Baseball Game

It's hard to learn how to play baseball, and it's hard to learn how to watch baseball. It's one of those hard things that the more you know about it, the more you learn about it, the more rewarding it is. . . . It's like listening to a piece of classical music. If you're only half paying attention, you probably only half enjoy it. If you're fully paying attention, you greatly enjoy it, but if you actually know something about music and musicology, then you'll really be able to enjoy it. I think that is the way it is with baseball.

—MICHAEL CHABON, "Pulitzer Prize-Winner's Unlikely Next Step," *Santa Rosa Press Democrat*, September 22, 2002

It is very difficult to spot and fully interpret signs, signals, and tip-offs, but watching the coaches and managers to see how information flows between players, the dugout, and the coaches' boxes is to see the inside game at work. "If you pay attention to the signs, you can learn a lot about the game," advised former player Harold Reynolds.

The best place to do this is at the ballpark because you can see the whole field and all the participants at a glance. Entering a ballpark invites one to coax meaning and detail from every nook and cranny of the place, from every pitch and play—and from the signals that set the stage for them. If you are close enough to watch the dugout or the coaches, you should be able to see signs being transmitted. Even in the outfield or bleachers you can see things that are missed by those in the box seats—for example, the signaling that commonly goes on behind infielders' backs to position the outfield or assign second-base coverage if a runner on first base attempts to steal.

It is generally harder to get a handle on the codes of the game from television for the simple reason that they are not as telegenic as, say, a batter spitting or adjusting his sweatbands. There is definitely an old-school aversion to television: "I think it's a mistake to televise baseball the way they're doing it today," *True* magazine quoted pioneering radio sportscaster Red Barber in its July 1971 issue. "All the instant replays and stop-action shots and slow-motion effects drive you to distraction. The continuity of the contest is destroyed. When I watch a baseball game on TV these days I get restless and irritated and pretty soon I turn it off. I don't have to take that kind of punishment."

Then there was this indictment: "Watching a baseball game on television is like chasing the great white whale in a goldfish bowl," novelist Ward Just wrote in 1984. "It trivializes everything: men two inches high, a ball the size of a bee. It is like looking at the heavens through a dime-store telescope." Even with today's ever-larger monster television screens and higher resolution, it still ain't the same.

To some, Barber's point may seem extreme and nothing more than an argument to "watch" the game on the radio, but to many there is an element of truth in what he says—especially as television becomes more and more a vehicle for advertising and the on-air commentary focuses on the promotion of ballpark giveaways. A few years back viewers of Washington Nationals games watched their team struggle as they were constantly reminded of an upcoming Calvin Coolidge bobblehead night. Many baseball fans with little interest in soccer were fascinated during the

2018 World Cup by a televised sport with huge blocks of time presented without ads for purple potency pills and spiced rum.

That said, the television viewer has a decided advantage because of the center-field camera, which is the key to the defensive game. "Fans at home should watch the catcher closely," said ESPN analyst Joe Morgan in a 2002 tutorial on watching baseball. "From the center-field camera angle, the catcher will indicate what pitch he is calling and what will—or should—happen on the next pitch. If the catcher sets up inside to any hitter, the pitch will be something hard—either a fastball or a slider. A pitcher will stay away from throwing changeups or slow curveballs inside. For a curveball pitcher the catcher will a lot of times set up over the middle of the plate instead of on the inside or outside corner."

Morgan's point is well taken, the only problem being that all televised games are not created equal and some directors hold back on the "setup" and cut to their center-field camera only as the ball is delivered. Morgan also warns that the center-field camera gives viewers a false sense of how hard it is to hit Major League pitching. "TV distorts how fast the ball gets from the pitcher's hand to homeplate. The ball appears to be going much slower because the camera shows the pitch from a wider angle."[1]

A general rule of thumb for those who want to extract everything they can from a visit to a ballpark is to start at the beginning and upon entering the park do precisely what the players do, which is to study the outfield flags to see how much wind there is and which way it's blowing. This can be an early indication of whether it's going to be a good day for hitters (wind blowing out) or a good day for pitchers (wind blowing in). Keep an eye on the thermometer. If it's a very hot afternoon, a ball will have a tendency to travel a long distance, compared to a cool evening, when the ball has less life. A very dry day will also help the ball travel.

The key to picking up signals at the ballpark is to watch the players, not the ball. The real strategic nuances of the game happen away from the ball. Fans are conditioned, by instinct and even more by television, to keep their eyes on either the pitcher, because he holds the ball, or the ball whenever it is hit. Instead, discipline yourself to watch anything but the ball; instead, watch the team at work, otherwise known as teamwork. Defensively, a well-coached team is worth watching for the constant adjusting and readjusting that is going on. Offensively, anyone who has ever watched the hit-and-run, squeeze bunt, or double steal put into play will recognize baseball for the complex team sport it is.

"On a long ball I watch the outfielders, not the ball," the late baseball historian and friend Bill Mead told me. "They will tell you where it is coming down. If you watch the ball you're going to miss out on the interplay between the outfielders." Sportscaster Red Barber once suggested that if you really wanted to "increase your baseball insight, as well as your pleasure," watch only one position for several innings at a stretch and see how the players on each club handle themselves. "Set your sights, say, on the third baseman, and watch nothing but the way he handles himself. Watch what he does in plays he isn't even in. Watch how he varies his fielding position to meet different situations. See the entire play of the game as the third baseman participates in it, or is prepared to even though nothing comes his way."[2]

Such a single-minded focus is crucial to your ability to see signs being given and especially to appreciate and possibly interpret their meaning. Spend a full inning or two watching nobody other than the third base coach or, if you can see into the dugout, the manager, and you will begin to recognize the game within the game, the intricate series of strategic decisions that revolve around every pitch.

Bring a pair of binoculars to the park. There are no unwritten rules against fans spying on the action, and binoculars help keep your attention focused in one place. You have time to do this. One of the great advantages of baseball is that it is played at a pace that allows time for the spectator to speculate on the next managerial decision before it happens. None other than the great Joe DiMaggio suggested this to a newspaper reporter who asked him how one should get the most out of watching a game. "By all means try to outguess the manager," he said in 1956, when he had become a spectator himself. "Don't wait for the pitch to see whether the batter will bunt, or try for the hit-and-run, or the catcher will call for a pitchout." DiMaggio added, "Take credit for master-minding the game with the guy sitting next to you. But be ready for his laughter when you second-guess wrong."[3]

Being at the ballpark allows one to pay attention to the inter-actions when the ball is *not* in play. Peter Gammons wrote, "In the 20-odd seconds between pitches, hands, feet, fingers, arms, eyes, caps, bats, gloves, clipboards and towels may all be moving in a silent clamor of signs."[4] Infielders will move in a direction to anticipate the most likely trajectory of the next pitch. The fan in the stands has the luxury of using these twenty seconds to project what may happen next, whereas the television viewer will likely see some celebrity in the box seats, a shot from an overhead blimp, or, more likely, a spot promoting an upcoming show.

An important thing to watch for during that twenty-second setup time is where the batter is looking before he steps into the batter's box. This is when the sign should be flashed from either of the base coaches or the dugout. If the batter waits until he is set up in the box before looking for a signal, he forces the coach to run through his signs in full view of the crowd and the opposition and loses an element of surprise. "Now everyone in the park knows something's up and I'm out there by myself telling everyone what's coming," third base coach Joey Amalfitano once explained.[5]

Also, pay attention to the batter during time-outs, especially one seemingly poised and ready for the pitch who steps out of the box to adjust his uniform, rub his hands together, or perhaps use his bat to knock dirt from his cleats. Although this could be a way to upset the pitcher, it is more likely an indication of a failure to communicate. Many years ago Connie Mack explained what was usually going on in his primer on the game, and the explanation still holds: "The chances are his cap hasn't been annoying him nor has the mud in his cleats; the real reason is that he has either missed the signal the coach is trying to relay to him, or the coach has suddenly canceled the signal previously given the batter and is telling him to wait until the signal can be relayed to him from the bench." When the batter steps back in the box, it can be assumed he has gotten a new signal.[6]

If, on the other hand, a batter calls time because there is something in his eye and he steps back and looks down, he may be trying to get an idea of where the catcher is setting up and what he is calling for. Such an obvious attempt to peek—in violation of the unwritten rule against looking back—will likely bring the next pitch high and inside.

While it is virtually impossible for a fan to decode a set of ever-changing signs that have been coded to prevent theft by men whose job it is to steal signs, there is a chance one can learn to spot a pitcher tipping off his pitch. This can be done by analyzing the position of his feet, the placement of his elbows, and any other conceivable variables and then connecting these to the pitches he throws. In 1993 Mets first base coach Barry Foote told a reporter, "Ninety percent of all pitchers tip off one or more of their pitches." Some would dispute the number, but it is still worth trying to pick from the stands.[7]

Also, keep an eye on the catcher. Some will inch forward after calling for a breaking ball to make it easier to catch the ball as it breaks low into the dirt. Keep an eye on the catcher's mitt, as it serves as a target for the pitcher.

If you are unable to spot telltale signs, appreciate the counter-measures, such as the size of the pitcher's glove. For example, pitchers who throw a split-fingered fastball need large gloves to keep their fingering of the ball hidden because the grip requires a splaying of the webbing of a traditional pitcher's glove. Buster Olney of the *New York Times* says that to mask his splitter, Roger Clemens played with a glove so large it could be confused with an outfielder's glove, and David Cone used a large plastic softball glove.

If one is absolutely determined to steal signs from the stands, consider an effort by *The Sporting News* to get how-to-steal advice from the experts. Managers and third base coaches advise patience and long-term concentration, suggesting that it is probably beyond the ability of those whose full-time job is not stealing signs. One manager said that it usually takes nine or ten games against the same opponent to see certain patterns, while another observed, "You have to concentrate to the exclusion of all else in the game. You can't allow yourself to 'watch the action' because the minute your attention wanders, you might miss the key to breaking the other team's code."[8]

Each situation during a game offers additional opportunities to see baseball's inner game in progress. With one or more runners on base, watch the actions of the shortstop and second baseman and of the catcher. Unless they have an automatic default agreement, the second baseman and the shortstop will alert the other as to who will cover second base in the event of a steal or pickoff attempt. Sometimes they will point behind their backs; other times they will signal behind their gloves with an open mouth, usually signifying that fielder will cover.

Pay attention to a runner on second, as he will, in all probability, be communicating with the man at bat. He may, for example, move his feet in such a way as to indicate the type or location of the pitch about to be pitched. In early 2002 Harold Reynolds gave a sign demonstration on ESPN. "If I led with my right, it was a fastball, and if I crossed over with my left foot it was an off-speed pitch, but if I didn't have the sign I would do a little shuffle," said Reynolds, explaining his former routine on the field. He was, in the meantime, using his arms to let the batter know the location of the pitch based on where the catcher was setting up.

Watch the dugout. Different parks have different angles of sight from one dugout to another. The old Shea Stadium in New York, for instance, was notorious for the fact that coaches could see from one dugout to the other. Managers will often place themselves in the least conspicuous corner of the dugout to keep from being seen as they send coded instructions. Be alert for any odd move or gesture by the manager or his dugout coach, who may be sitting next to him relaying signals. The coach may simply cross his arms or put his hands behind his head to transmit a signal whispered to him by the manager. "Some clubs send signs with different grips on a fungo bat, covering or wrapping hands around the knob, for example," Jimmy Bragan told a reporter when he coached for the Brewers. "You can use your head or foot, too, to pass along a signal."[9]

However, make no absolute assumptions as to who is really giving the signs because anyone on the field can be relaying them. Even the pros can pick the wrong man. Terry Bevington, when he served as the Toronto Blue Jays' first base coach, told about the time he was in Chicago and was told by Gene Tenace, who was then third base coach in Toronto, that "he had picked up my steal sign. I thought that was rather odd because that year the steal sign always went through the first-base coach." For a while when he was managing in Oakland, Tony LaRussa used his trainer to flash signals, and there is at least one modern example of a mascot giving signs: former Major League manager Jack McKeon was once ejected from a Minor League game and returned in the mascot's uniform to give signs.

The hands of base coaches also offer clues. If a coach points to a base, he's ordering the runner to stop there, while a beckoning move means to keep coming. The third base coach will come down the line thirty or forty feet toward home plate when the ball is hit into the outfield because from this standpoint he can see the whole field and better direct traffic. A bobble or bad throw allows him to direct the runners to take extra bases. A third base coach who seems fluid in tossing off signs and then slows down his cadence may be making sure his batter or base runner gets the message. If a runner on first glances back at the first base coach, it is quite likely that he is looking for instructions in the form of a sign.

The umpires, too, have their inner language. Besides their established and public signs—out, safe, fair or foul, time, play—they communicate with one another nonverbally. A prime example is when one member of the crew signals the others that the infield-fly rule is in effect. It varies from crew to crew, but one common method is for the umpire at second base to touch the brim of his hat with his thumb up and then give a thumbs-up signal to the plate umpire, who responds with a similar unobtrusive thumb motion.

Umpires are constantly checking with the other members of their crew. If, for example, you see an umpire make a cutting motion across his throat or tap his right pant leg with a closed right fist, he is probably asking for the number of outs from the plate umpire, who may signal the number by touching the side of his mask with a closed fist (no outs) or one finger or two fingers extended.

The relationship between the batter and the plate umpire can also be interesting to watch. A batter is supposed to voice any complaints to the umpire without turning to look at him, thus not tipping off fans to the dispute and thereby attempting to turn the crowd against the umpire. "Never turn around," John Mizerock, 2002 bullpen coach of the Kansas City Royals, says. "You can holler and pretty much say what you want as long as you are facing the pitcher." Journalist Tim Kurkjian has written, as a corollary, "As a pitcher, if an ump misses a pitch down the middle, do what Hall of Famer Fergie Jenkins used to do: don't even flinch, just keep on pitching. As good as umpires are, they're human. If you embarrass them, they'll embarrass you." They won't give you a close call, or they'll call you out on a bad pitch if you make them look bad.

A Glossary of Signs, Signals, and Tip-Offs

activator   A sign telling the player to proceed with the designated play; a green light.

automatic switch   Reversing the meaning of a sign or signs when it becomes apparent they are being stolen. Don Drysdale told Ross Newhan of the *Los Angeles Times*, "The best way to stop [the stealing of signs] is to have an automatic switch. When the catcher puts down a curve, throw the fastball. If the hitter is leaning over the plate, expecting the curve, that can get his attention in a hurry." A classic example of the automatic switch takes place when the catcher gives a normal sign but then puts his bare hand on top of his mitt to call for the opposite.

block signals   Signals that use the coach's body as a map, with each section, or "block," having a different meaning. For example, the body is often divided into four sections, with each having a different meaning if touched. Holding hands above the belt or below the belt designates two different blocks.

bobble-head   Name for a pitcher who is given to shaking off—or pretending to do so—pitches called for by his catcher in order to confuse the batter.

braille-man   A coach skilled at sending signs and hand signals to base runners. Most signs involve use of the hands.

call   1. *n.* An umpire's stated or signaled ruling on a pitch (ball, strike, balk, foul ball, or hit batsman) or a play (safe or out). 2. *n.* The catcher's signal for a specific pitch. 3. *n.* The manager's decision on a starting pitcher or his signal to the bullpen for a relief pitcher or for a relief pitcher to begin warming up. 4. *v.* To make an umpiring decision.

combination signal   Two or more motions tied together to represent one sign; for instance, "skin and skin" (touching the face and then the chin) might be the real sign, but "skin, color, skin" (touching the face, touching red lettering, and then touching the chin) would be nothing more than three decoys. More complicated than most signs. St. Louis baseball writer Bob Broeg once said of combination signals that they "are missed more easily than flash signs and are more likely to be intercepted."

cutoff sign   Usually a simple instruction on the part of the third baseman to the shortstop to either "cut it off" or "let it go," a message that can be signaled either by voice or with a simple hand sign. The third baseman, who is watching the fielded ball come in from the outfield, must determine where the best play can be made.

dead zone   A signal given to let the recipient know that the next sign—normally a legitimate indicator or action sign—is a fake. It is intended to cross up sign stealers.

decoy, or dummy, signal   A sign, or signal, from the catcher, dugout, or coach's box that is meaningless and meant only to mislead and confuse those trying to steal the signal.

deek/deke   To mislead with bogus signals; baseball slang for "decoy."

deuce   The curveball, so called because the basic sign for that pitch, at every level from the sandlot to the Majors, is two fingers down at the thigh.

finger system   The system of communication by which the catcher signals a suggested pitch to the pitcher by flashing the fingers on his bare hand. From the crouched position, the catcher gives the finger signals between his legs to keep the batter from seeing them. Some catchers put white adhesive tape on their fingers so they can be better seen from the mound. Traditionally, one finger is given for a fastball, two for a curveball, and three for an off-speed pitch. William G. Brandt (*Baseball Magazine*, October 1932) wrote of three fingers: "[It] can be almost anything, screwball, forkball, knuckleball, slop-ball, squib, dipsy-dew."

first-letter system   A system in which the first letter in the name of an object touched matches the first letter of the sign. For example, a touch of the hat will call a hit-and-run, a touch of the belt is a call for a bunt, and a touch of the shirt is for a steal.

flap   A catcher-pitcher system based on the sign given after a number of fingers have been thrown, with the flap being the activator.

flash   1. *n.* A signal given only once and quickly, such as a tug of the belt. In *The Complete Baseball Handbook*, Walter Alston points out that the trouble with flash signals is that they are so easily missed. He suggests a preliminary sign telling the batter that a flash is coming, as well as another telling him there will be no signal. 2. *v.* To give signals quickly in the hope that one's opponents cannot steal them.

flash system   A system of communication dependent on quick moves that seem to merge into one.

flip   To change the meaning of a finger sign to confuse sign stealers and, perhaps, draw batters into harm's way. If two fingers is the call for a curveball, after the flip two fingers signifies a fastball.

go sign/go signal   A sign given by a base coach to a base runner to get him to attempt to steal or advance to the next base. One of the most important signs in a coach's repertoire is the verbal signal to go, which is given when a base runner advances or scores after a fly ball has been caught. The coach must time this perfectly in order to send the runner at the precise moment that the ball is being caught. This is so adroitly practiced in Major League Baseball that it is the rare fan who has ever seen a runner called out for leaving third before the ball is caught. At the end of World War II this term was used metaphorically for the conversion of the nation from a wartime to a civilian economy. A headline in the *San Francisco Examiner* for August 15, 1945, read, "Truman Flashes 'Go' Signal on Reconversion."

grass puller A first base coach, or third base coach in the early part of the twentieth century, whose method of transmitting signs was to pull grass. Hughie Jennings and Arlie Latham were two coaches who turned grass pulling into part of a coaching sideshow. Its first use was in July 1908 in *Baseball Magazine.*

green light 1. A coach's sign flashed to a batter allowing him to swing. It is most commonly given on a 3-0 count. *See also* "hit sign." 2. A go sign given to a base runner to take an extra base or attempt to steal, at the discretion of the base runner. Keith Hernandez (*Pure Baseball*, 1994) writes, "Speed has changed all the old thinking about base stealing. The quick guys have a permanent green light. When they get a jump, they can go." *Compare* "red light"; "stop sign." 3. President Franklin D. Roosevelt's letter of January 15, 1942, to Commissioner Kenesaw Mountain Landis to continue playing baseball during World War II. The president wrote in response to Landis's offer to cancel baseball: "If 300 teams use 5,000 or 6,000 players, these players are a definite recreational asset to at least 20,000,000 of their fellow citizens and that in my judgment is thoroughly worthwhile." FDR does not actually use the words "green light" in the letter, which was immediately given that nickname. *Etymology*: An obvious borrowing from the green light of traffic control.

hit sign   The sign that allows the batter to swing if the pitch looks good, used in tandem with the take sign.

hog-wild runner   A determined base runner who often ignores the coach's signs or is intent on reaching the next base. "On nearly every ball club, there are some players who are known in the frank parlance of the profession as 'hog wild runners.' The expression means that these players are bitten by a sort of 'bug' which causes them to lose their heads when once they get on the bases. They cannot be stopped, oftentimes fighting with a coacher to go on to the next base, when it is easy to see that if the attempt is made, the runner is doomed" (Christy Mathewson, *Pitching in a Pinch*).

holding signal/holding sign   A sign that is activated when it is held longer than all the other signs, sometimes for several seconds; especially suited for less experienced players. It can be as simple as doffing one's cap for a few seconds or a bending an elbow. Walter Alston says in his *Complete Baseball Handbook* that it is the simplest to receive because it is held long enough for "the message to sink in," adding, "A player can look more than once if he is in doubt about the signal." For the same reason that it is one of the easiest to understand, it is also one of the easiest to steal.

hot sign   The actual "live" sign embedded in decoys and following an activator or indicator.

indicator   Sign telling the player that a "live" sign is forthcoming. Not all indicators are hand signs. For instance, under one common system if the coach is standing at the far end of the coach's box, the signals are on, but if he is standing at the near end of the box, they are off.

individual sign   A sign sent to one player and not the others. This can be as simple as looking away from the player to whom the signal is being given.

inside signal   Catcher's signs from inside the thigh.

key The sign that unlocks the active signal; the indicator. According to a 1984 *Baseball Digest* article, Joe Torre, in his role as Mets manager, would "'key' his signs by spitting in different directions."

long ball Jim Brosnan (*The Long Season*, 1960) wrote that the term is "often used as a nickname for catchers who signal for too many bad pitches," allowing the batter to hit the long ball, or home run.

missed sign/missed signal Any communications miscue on the field. It is a major cause of errors and can have a serious impact on the outcome of a game. Even veteran players and coaches are susceptible. In a game against the Twins on May 20, 2001, Cal Ripken Jr. was given a bunt sign on 1-1 and 2-1 with a runner on first. He took both for balls, and then manager Mike Hargrove took the bunt sign off and relayed the message to the third base coach, Tom Trebelhorn, who thought he relayed it to Ripken. But the veteran did not get the sign correctly and laid down the perfect bunt and moved the runner to second. After the game Hargrove noted that, despite the outcome, Ripken had "missed a sign."

mnemonic signs Using a simple set of words whose first letters stand for the an instruction. The mnemonic "Thomas Baker High School" stands for "take," "bunt," and "hit-and-run" and then signals the corresponding number for the call—in this case 3, for "hit-and-run."

odd/even system A system of signs used by the catcher (especially when a runner is on second base and presumably looking for a specific sign) in which three signs are flashed for each pitch. For example, if the number of fingers flashed adds up to an even number, a fastball (traditionally represented by one finger) is called for; if they add up to an odd number, a curveball (traditionally two fingers) is called for; and if the fingers are cupped at the end of the sequence,

an off-speed pitch may be ordered. All of this can, of
course, be reversed.

offensive signs   Take, bunt, hit-and-run, steal, squeeze,
and no steal are the conventional six signs employed by
third base coaches. In addition, there are signs for special
situations—such as the proposed double steal, with the
object of getting the man in from third base in a first-and-
third situation—and signs giving the batter or runner the
option of making a play if he thinks he can make it work.

open mouth/closed mouth signs   A common method used
to communicate between the second baseman and the
shortstop in determining who will cover second base in
case the runner at first attempts a steal. The player signals
by putting his glove in front of his face and turning his head
toward the second baseman or shortstop to hide the signs
from the coach. Normally, an open mouth means the shortstop will cover, and a closed mouth means it will be up to
the second baseman.

option sign/optional sign   A sign suggesting to a batter or
runner that a possibility exists. Don Leppert, third base
coach for the Houston Astros in the early 1980s, was an
advocate of such signs. In a 1982 interview he said, "I can
give an 'optional' sign, which means I feel the third baseman is playing too far back and for the batter to bunt if he
feels comfortable in doing so. Now this is not a mandatory
sign, it's just a suggestion on my part based upon something I may have observed that the batter may have missed.
Also, say in a situation with runners at first and third, I can
signal the bunt in such a way that it means we are primarily
interested in moving the runner from first to second, but if
the man at third feels the bunt can make it through, he can
try for the plate."

outside signals   Signals transmitted by a catcher from outside the thigh. Some catchers avoid the traditional inside

signals in favor of these. Eddie Yost once described the late Thurmon Munson of the Yankees as a perfect example of the outside signer, meaning that "everything he does— touching his mask, shin guard, picking up dirt—is a sign."

peeker   A batter in the batter's box who turns his head back to attempt to see the catcher's signs or where he is positioning himself or holding his mitt as a target. The tactic of peeking is not against any written rule, but as an unwritten rule it ranks high. In 2013 Cincinnati manager Dusty Baker recalled a time during his playing days when he was blushingly caught in the act. "Johnny Bench caught me peeking," Baker said. "I looked back and saw him looking right up at me. He said, 'Merry Christmas, Dusty.' I thought, 'Uh, oh.' I said, 'Merry Christmas, Johnny.'"

pickoff sign   Sign that a pickoff play is about to be attempted. These come in several varieties. The most common one is between the catcher and the first baseman with a man on first. A catcher might glance at first and then knead the back of his mitt to signal the pickoff. The first baseman might then simply tug his belt to acknowledge the signal and let the catcher know that he will arrive when the ball is thrown to the bag. The communication for a pickoff at second exemplifies the usefulness of signs. Typically, the shortstop sets the sign—say, a clenching of his fist or a pounding of his glove with his bare hand. From the instant the sign is sent, the pitcher and the shortstop begin to count. At the count of three the shortstop heads for the bag, and at four the pitcher whirls around, stepping off the rubber in the process, and fires the ball to the bag. If this all works, the runner is out on the count of five.

pickpocket   Sign stealer.

pump system   A method of signaling in which the number of signals given is the signal and the nature of the signal means nothing. A coach might use one sign for the bunt, two for the hit-and-run, three for take, and four for no sign—essentially a decoy. For a catcher it is the number of times his fingers are thrown and not the fingers that are thrown. A variation on this, pioneered by Leo Durocher while managing the Giants, was to count only the pumps thrown with the coach's right hand, while all those thrown with the left were decoys. *Compare* "finger system."

release sign   A sign that allows a player to look away from the signal giver. The purpose of a release sign is to make sure that the receiver does not look away the moment the "action sign" is given, hence giving it away. A common practice is to hold the receiver's attention while decoy signs are being sent until the sender signs off with a clap of the hands. Some players do not need any help in this department. "Pee Wee Reese probably was the best player I have seen at receiving signals," his former skipper Walter Alston said of him. "After I gave him a sign, he would just keep looking and looking. The first couple of times, I was not sure whether he got the signs or not, but in his own way, he was decoying to keep the other club from knowing the sign was given."

repeat sign   A separate sign to repeat the call on back-to-back offensive plays or pitches. Andy Lopez writes in his book *Coaching Baseball Successfully*: "Repeating the same sign over and over enables your opponent to try to interpret the sign, anticipating your offensive strategy. By having a simple repeat sign, your offensive players will understand that the strategy on the previous pitch will he repeated on the next pitch. The repeat sign can be as simple as touching a certain part of your body that's considered an automatic sign."

rockhead   A player who misses signs, according to Bill McCullough in the *Brooklyn Eagle*, September 3, 1937.

rub-off sign   A sign that cancels all previous live signs. Used, for example, to call off a hit-and-run play when a pitchout is sensed by the manager or third base coach. A batter will use the rub-off when there is confusion or an inability to understand the rationale behind a signal. Same as a "wipe-off sign."

selling the call   The process by which an umpire makes a call and underscores it with flair and authority. Gesture, body language, and voice all contribute, as does each umpire's own personal sense of rhythm and style.

shake-off   *n.* The act of indicating a refusal from a pitcher to a catcher who has called for a specific pitch. Shake-offs underscore a difference in approach between the two.

shake off   *v.* To reject a proposed pitch, usually by the shaking of the pitcher's head. Some pitchers shake off a sign with another gesture, such as a move of the glove. *Syn*: "throw off."

shake the catcher around   For a pitcher to shake off all the signs and return to the original sign. Joe Garagiola (*Baseball Is a Funny Game*) explained: "A pitcher does that to confuse the hitter as to what the pitcher is going to throw." Buster Olney, who covered the Yankees for the *New York Times*, reported that Mariano Rivera had been known to accept the pitch and then shake his head eight or nine times just to confuse the batter.

sign   1. *n.* A secret motion, gesture, or sound that conveys information, such as the flashing fingers of a catcher or the motions of another player, coach, or manager. A catcher employs signs constantly in calling for specific pitches from the pitcher. A coach uses them to call for offensive plays, such as bunts and steals. *Syn*: "signal"; "wig-wag." First use, 1888. "As to the question of 'signs.' Every battery, by which is meant a pitcher and catcher, must have a perfectly understood private code of signals, so that they may make known their intentions and wishes to another without at the same time apprising the opposing players. . . . Until within a few years this sign was always given by the pitcher, but now it is almost the universal practice for the catcher to give it to the pitcher, and if the latter doesn't want to pitch the ball asked for he changes the sign by a shake of the head" (John Montgomery Ward, *Base-Ball: How to Become a Player*). 2. *v.* To send a signal. "I wanted to give him a spitter but Schalk signs me for the fast one and I give it to him" (Ring W. Lardner, *You Know Me Al*).

signal   1. *n. Syn:* "sign." 2. *v.* To make a sign.

sign-stealing   A tactic by which a team spots and deciphers its opponent's signs. For this reason teams work to keep their signs as cryptic and confusing as possible. With a runner at second base, the pitcher and catcher usually change signs because the catcher's signs to the pitcher are clearly visible to the batting team. Some have attached great significance to the practice.

sign system   An assortment of signs that includes these components: an indicator, a wipe-off, an activator, a release sign, and many decoys.

steal   To detect and interpret the opposition's signs.

stop sign   A coach's signal to hold up a base runner from advancing. It is usually no more complicated than a hand upraised to stop a runner. It is one of the few signs that has been routinely disobeyed without serious repercussions to the violator. Perhaps the most famous example was the "Mad Dash" made by St. Louis Cardinals Hall of Famer Enos Slaughter to win the 1946 World Series from the Boston Red Sox. With the Series tied at 3–3 and the seventh game tied at 3–3, Slaughter opened the bottom of the eighth inning with a single. Two outs later, with Harry Walker at bat, he was still at first. Slaughter took off for second in an attempted steal, and Walker hit the ball into center field. Third base coach Mike Gonzalez signaled for Slaughter to stop, but he ran through the sign and beat the throw from the cutoff man, sliding into home with what proved to be the winning run. Cardinals great Stan Musial later insisted that Slaughter "outran" the ball to win the Series. In 1999 a statue depicting the slide was dedicated at Busch Stadium in St. Louis—tribute to a man running a stop sign.

take sign   Sign to the batter instructing him not to swing at the next pitch, usually given when the count is in his favor (2-0, 3-0, or 3-1) and the team is in need of runs. Sometimes the take sign is removed when a player is establishing a hitting streak. "When I was in my fifty-six game hitting streak in 1941," Joe DiMaggio wrote in *Baseball for Everyone*, "Joe McCarthy played right along with me and never gave me the take sign once."

tell   A gesture or small change in behavior that signals whether the next pitch will be, for example, a breaking ball or a fastball. The term comes from poker, where players try to determine the strength of an opponent's hand by his or her behavior—such as an ear-to-ear relaxed smile, indicating a strong hand.

thief   Honorific reserved for the most adroit sign stealers and base stealers.

throw-over sign   A signal, usually from the dugout, instructing the pitcher to throw to a runner on first who seems to be a threat to steal.

tip-off   An unconscious sign in the form of a mannerism given by pitchers, catchers, or other players that can sometimes be read by a canny manager, coach, or player to foretell a pitch or a play.

tip of the cap   Baseball has a separate set of signs for the spectator. The most common is the tip of the cap given by a player who has been accorded an ovation from the fans. Sometimes the tip of the cap can be turned around as a mark of grace. On a particularly nasty night in Cleveland, which was also Game Five of the 1998 American League Championship Series, the local fans taunted Yankee pitcher

David Wells with remarks about his late mother, Eugenia, and then booed him when he left the game in the eighth inning. He responded with a tip of his cap.

traffic signs Overt hand signals for stop and go, used by coaches to direct runners. Coaches introduced these traffic signals—a hand upraised to stop a runner and a wave of the arm to move him along—in the first decade of the twentieth century to counter defenders who were shouting bogus instructions

touching signs Most common form of sign transmission from a coach or manager: touching colors (drawing a hand across the letters of a uniform shirt or touching the colored part of a sock), touching flesh, or touching the cap. Tugging signs, such as tugging at the belt, are considered part of this system.

umpiring signal One of a simple set of hand and arm movements that an umpire uses to indicate calls. For example, a raised right arm with a clenched fist along the base paths means that the runner is out, while an emphatic horizontal crossing of the hands with the palms down indicates the runner is safe, and a raised right arm at the plate indicates a called strike.

wave on A coach's signal to a runner to continue to the next base.

wig-wag Synonym of a sign in the early days of baseball, from the system of signal flags and torches employed in the Civil War that was dubbed "wig-wag."

wig-wagger A base coach.

wipe-off sign A sign that negates every live or active sign flashed to that point. Same as a rub-off sign.

wooden Indian A base coach who does not give a signal to a base runner. Derived from the impassive image of the carved wooden American Indian traditionally placed in front of cigar stores.

word signal   Signal contained in a coach's phrasing. For instance, the word "have" could be the signal for a hit-and-run. "Let's have a big inning" might be the signal to the man on base, and he might then yell to the batter, "Here's where we have the rally." The conventional wisdom is that the problem with a word code is that coaches place unconscious stress on the code word, and it is easily stolen. There have been bizarre systems over the years that have fueled comic anecdotes. In the 1920s a man named Mickey Devine was the player-manager for the Minor League club in Newark. He decided to initiate a new system. If he called out the name of a city west of the Mississippi, he was signaling for a sacrifice, but if the city was east of the river he was ordering a hit-and-run. One afternoon Devine got on first and shouted "Waxahachie," the name of a town in Texas. The batter shook his head, and Devine repeated it several times, until the batter threw down his bat and said, "Can't you say New York or San Francisco?" Baseball historian John B. Holway first told the author of Leo Durocher in Japan in 1962 deciding to give his signs in English and then finding out after a couple of his players were thrown out that the catcher was a graduate of the University of Hawaii.

ACKNOWLEDGMENTS

Most of the interviews conducted for the first edition of this book were conducted between March 2001 and August 2002. As a practical matter this means that position and team identities of those quoted are frozen in time. I thank the following managers, coaches, players, and baseball writers for their time, most of which was given during spring training: Roger Angell, the *New Yorker*; Yogi Berra, New York Yankees spring training instructor; Terry Bevington, Toronto Blue Jays third base coach; Larry Bowa, Philadelphia Phillies; George Brett, vice president for baseball operations Kansas City Royals; Dave Clark, hitting coach Pittsburgh Pirates; Terry Crowley, Baltimore Orioles hitting coach; Rich Dauer, Kansas City Royals 3rd base coach; Rick Dempsey, first base coach Baltimore Orioles; Larry Derker, manager Houston Astros; Mike Easler, hitting instructor Cincinnati Reds; Tom Gamboa, first base coach Kansas City Royals; Dallas Green, senior adviser to the general manager Philadelphia Phillies; Greg Gross, hitting coach Philadelphia Phillies; Mike Hargrove, Baltimore Orioles manager; Billy Hatcher, third base coach Tampa Bay Devil Rays; Elrod Hendricks, Baltimore Orioles bullpen coach; Reggie Jackson, New York Yankees spring training instructor; Lamar Johnson, Kansas City Royals hitting coach; Dave Kelly, Library of Congress; Howard Kleinberg, Cox News Service; Tim Kurkjian, ESPN; Tony LaRussa, St. Louis Cardinals manager; Fred Manfra, Baltimore Orioles broadcaster; Charlie Manual, Cleveland Indians; Buck Martinez, manager Toronto Blue Jays; Don Mattingly, spring training instructor New York Yankees; broadcaster Ed Michaels; John Mizerock, bullpen coach Kansas City Royals; Mickey Morandini with the 2001 Toronto Blue Jays; Tony Muser, manager Kansas City Royals; Tim Naehring, director of player development Cincinnati Reds; Jerry Narron, third base coach Texas Rangers; Buster Olney, as a Yankees beat writer for the *New York Times*; Sam Perlozzo, Baltimore Orioles bench coach; Bill Plummer III, Hall of Fame manager; Alonzo Powell, hitting coach AA Chattanooga of Cincinnati Reds; Mickey Rivers, New York Yankees spring training instructor; Leon Roberts, Cincinnati Reds hitting coordinator; Bill Robinson, coach Florida Marlins; Tommy Sandt, first base coach Pittsburgh Pirates; Bob Schaefer, Kansas City Royals bench coach; Dan Shaughnessy, *Boston Globe*; Dave Smith, Project Retrosheet; Bruce Tanner, bullpen coach Pittsburgh Pirates; Syd Thrift, Baltimore Orioles vice president of baseball operations; Jeff Torberg, manager Florida Marlins; Joe Torre, manager New York Yankees; John Vukovich, third base coach Philadelphia Phillies; Willie Weinbaum, ESPN; and Don Zimmer, bench coach New York Yankees.

I would also like to thank a group of friends and associates who have helped me collect information, find leads, and otherwise act as friends of this project: Lane Akers; David W. Anderson, SABR; John G. Arrison, librarian and archivist at the Penobscot Marine Museum, Searsport, Maine; Robert Dudley; Bill Francis, National Baseball Hall of Fame Library; Joseph C. Goulden; Dan Gutman; Mim Harrison; John Holway; Kevin P. Kerr; Bob Luke; Tom Mann, Library of Congress; David Martel; Skip McAfee; Andy McCue; Joe McGillen, SABR; the late William B. Mead; Tom Mellers; Peter Morris, SABR; the late Robert F. Perkins; Ross Reader for her knowledge of cricket; the late Ray Robinson for his thoughts on the events of 1951; Norman Stevens; Stephen Wells; and David L. "Navy Dave" Woods of Middleway, West Virginia, captain, U.S. Navy.

For help with the second edition I would like to thank the following: Marty Appel, Jeff Chamberlin, David Sheinen, Barry Svergula, and Frank Vaccaro.

NOTES

Prologue

1. It's 258 feet versus 297 at Ebbets Field and 296 at Yankee Stadium.

Introduction

1. Mark Gonzales, "Cubs Manager Joe Maddon Admits to Sign-Stealing during Coaching Days," *Chicago Tribune*, February 19, 2018.
2. Russell, "How Stengel Handles Sign-Stealers," 65–66.
3. Monteleone, *Branch Rickey's Little Blue Book*, 50–51.
4. Durslag, "When the Coach Rubs His Arm," 27.
5. James, *Bill James Historical Baseball Abstract*, 20, 23; James, *The Baseball Book, 1991*, sketch of Jimmy Archer, 341.
6. Frank Dell, "White Broke Mold as Red Sox Catcher," *Boston Globe*, August 7, 1991, 33. Occasionally, a battery does not work well together. Such a case existed in 1934 with the St. Louis Cardinals. It seems that Dizzy Dean proclaimed that he had no faith in catcher Spud Davis and told anyone who would listen that he did not want to pitch to him. Yet Dean won thirty games that year, and the Cardinals won the pennant. What Dean did not know was that Frankie Frisch, player-manager of the team, was actually calling all the pitches from his perch on second base.
7. Brosnan, *Pennant Race*, 250
8. Tebbetts, "I'd Rather Catch," 2, of the online version of this article, which appears in the flashbacks section of the magazine's website, http://www.theatlantic.com.
9. Tom Swope's unpaginated manuscript on Dressen was found in the Dressen file at the National Baseball Library in Cooperstown. Swope was on the staff of the *Cincinnati Post*.
10. Falls, "Master at Sign Stealing," 85.

11. Bakalar, *The Baseball Fan's Companion*, 100–101.
12. Coffin, *Old Ball Game*, 70; Deindorfer, "Baseball's Counter-spies," 73.
13. Abramson, "Larceny on the Diamond," 20.
14. Mathewson, *Pitching in a Pinch*, 306.

1. Signal Flags and Torches

1. Preface to *International Code of Signals* (Washington DC: Defense Mapping Agency, 1969), iii–iv. Then as now, these signals could be bone simple—*A* for "I have a diver down," *O* for "Man overboard," and *Y* for "I am dragging my anchor."
2. Even today there are professions that deal in silent hand signals—heavy equipment operators, underwater divers, surveyors, and hotel doormen who signal cabbies as to fares and their destinations.
3. The Morse code is not really a code at all but an alphabet, easily encoded.
4. A private maritime code book in the possession of the Penobscot Marine Museum in Searsport, Maine, attests to the point. This code is based on plain English so that a shipowner who got the message PELTMONGER would know, "This vessel has arrived in serious distress at . . . ," and if it was followed by HOGHERD he would know it was in Boston. Should one's commercial rivals intercept the message, they would have no inkling of what was happening—that is, unless they had stolen your code book
5. Baseball management had its own codes used to save money and ensure secrecy. Dave Kelly of the Library of Congress discovered a copy of *The Private Telegraphic Code of the National Association of Professional Baseball Leagues* (1933), which works like this: An owner wanting to send the message "John Wilson accepted our terms three hundred dollars February thirteenth six o'clock. Contract was signed February twenty-fifth" would use the code book and send this: "John Wilson Pactolian Aggressed Acclimate Gelding Hardiest. Galbast Genevan."
6. "The Excelsior vs. Flour City Base Ball Clubs," *Rochester (NY) Evening Express*, July 9, 1860, 30. This item was discovered by baseball historian Priscilla Astifan in her documentation of the history of Rochester baseball of the period 1858–77. This was the only reference to signals that she can recall in her exhaustive research into this early period.
7. E-mail correspondence from Dr. David L. Woods, July 2002, captain, U.S. Navy (retired), an expert on the history of signals whose

dissertation was entitled "The Development of Visual Signal Systems on Land and Sea" and who is the author of *A History of Tactical Communication Techniques* (1965).

8. In a note written on December 5, 2002, David Woods explains: Polybius invented at least two rather different torch signal systems. The first dealt with messages pre-carved on a stick floated in a water jug. A torch told the other signal party when to turn on & off the water in their identical jug—so the correct message on the stick would be in the correct place at the second torch. The better system involved more torches plus the Greek alphabet on a bingo card-like grid five spaces across & five down. Obviously, this was slower—since messages had to be spelled out. But it allowed for more than half a dozen messages (or whatever the limit of a stick was). Thinking today, one might wonder why there were not 25 numbered sticks—each with the same 5 messages carved in them? This could expand the message vocabulary to 125 messages vs. half-a-dozen.

9. Carrying the system in a backpack was a bit of an exaggeration used to sell the system. Surely, this could be done with flags the size of modern two-flag semaphore signals. But the wig-wag flags were usually on polls ten feet long. The folded flags were in the backpack, but the poles were probably cut from saplings at the site of the signal station.

10. Woods, *History of Tactical Communication*, 84.

11. Woods, *History of Tactical Communication*, 85. Despite aberrations like Hooker, the importance of signs and signals was underscored again on both sides during the conflict, ending with the signals being used to offer surrender at Appomattox and for signal torches flashed early in the morning of April 15, 1865, from Washington DC to all local stations: "Instruct your pickets to arrest every man who comes near or attempts to pass from the city. The President is killed." Woods, *History of Tactical Communication*, 88. Historian John Allen Krout concluded, "The intersectional movements of the armies tended to nationalize baseball." Krout, *Annals of American Sport*, 119.

12. Discovered by baseball writer Peter Morris, who found it reprinted in *The Ball Player's Chronicle*, August 22, 1867.

13. Novelist Darryl Brock, who discovered this highly significant citation in research for his novel *If I Never Get Back*, which deals in detail with the '69 Red Stockings and their style of baseball, told me:

I can't add anything to that *Alta* account, but I do know that Harry Wright employed defensive shifts, and the Cincinnatis were regarded, then and later, as fielding wizards. Without an infield fly rule, they plagued opposing runners by dropping pop-ups to enable double plays—or, if the runner was in motion, catching it and doubling him off the bag he left; George Wright was an acknowledged master of this. Likewise, catcher Doug Allison would intentionally drop third strikes with a runner on first, fire the ball to second to initiate a DP, and leave the batter still at the plate looking around in confusion. Harry Wright also had his "strikers" hit to specific locations rather than just slug away. I imagine that signs, vocal or otherwise, might have been used in all of these maneuvers, but have not come across source material to document it. "Inside" coverage was still a few decades or more away, unfortunately.

Addressing the question of why this description appeared in California, Brock surmises: "Papers outside the eastern cities offered the best views of [the Redlegs], hence the nice San Francisco coverage. In New York, Philly etc. they were familiar figures, and writers did not detail them the way smaller towns or distant cities might."

14. Dickson, *New Dickson Baseball Dictionary*, 53. Henry Chadwick calls the battery the "main attacking force of the little army of nine players in the field in a contest."

15. Daniel, "Daniel Traces Signal-Swiping History," 15.

16. Ward, *Base-Ball*, 73–75.

17. *Sporting Life* for February 27, 1892, for instance, says:

Hoy possesses far more than the average brightness, and taught the finger alphabet to the players so thoroughly that they spoke it among themselves on the team, and when they had a grievance against the Boss and he was within ear shot they gave him a quiet warning in the finger language. Based on his achievements, many fans are today lobbying for Hoy's election to the Hall of Fame. In 1961, six months short of his 100th birthday, he threw out the first ball for Game 3 of the World Series between the Reds and the Yankees. Annoyed with the sportswriters at the event who called him William Hoy he proclaimed, "Tell them to call me Dummy again, like always." Hoy was an amateur baseball historian with an eye for the bizarre and in his 99th year wrote to Hall of Fame historian Lee Allen with the gleeful news that

he found evidence of a baseball game played in 1858 which was
called after five innings because a player was "completely filled
with gas and unable to continue."

Ed Dundon was the first in the game. Baseball historian Peter Morris notes that Dundon was nearly stabbed to death by a soldier
during the 1883 season who took his silence as insolence. Dundon, a
right-handed pitcher, played Major League ball for Columbus in the
American Association in 1883 and 1884.

18. *Washington DC Evening Star*, April 7, 1888. "When [Hoy] bats a man
stands in the Captain's box near third base and signals to him decisions of the umpire on balls and strikes by raising his fingers." Discovered by Bill Deane in his work on the Hoy legend.

19. The Fumess quote appears on a website (http://www.dummyhoy
.com) devoted to Hoy and efforts to support his induction into the
Baseball Hall of Fame.

20. Salsinger, "Connie Originated Signals," 28.

21. Pfeffer, *Scientific Ball*, 18. This rare book depicts a game that is a far
cry from the laconic rural pastime that many today assume characterized the nineteenth-century game.

22. Pfeffer, *Scientific Ball*, 15–20.

23. *Detroit Tribune*, March 16, 1905, from an unpaginated clipping in the
Cross file at the National Baseball Library.

24. Ward's comments appear in the 1896 edition of Spalding's *Official
Baseball Guide*. Rickey quote from Monteleone, *Branch Rickey's Little Blue Book*, 50.

25. In Frank Graham's 1944 biography of McGraw, he quoted from
Sporting Life, May 9, 1891, 2: "Sam Wise has the Baltimores working
under one of the most complete code of signals in the Association."

2. The Buzzer and Binocular Era

1. Dittmar, "A Shocking Discovery." See also Grayson, "They Really
Stole Signs Then," 68.

2. The term "vibrathrob" is the classic nonce word that only seems to
be used in the retelling of this story.

3. Joe Dittmar, whose definitive article on this subject, "A Shocking
Discovery," appeared in the 1991 *Baseball Research Journal*, tracks
Chiles after the incident:

Following a shocking season with the Phillies in 1900, Chiles was
arrested during the off season in a con artist scheme and sen-

tenced to two years of hard labor on a prison farm in Huntsville, Texas. He served less than sixteen months, however, and not because of good behavior. On August 15, 1902, Chiles escaped from the Texas Department of Corrections. In the last known sliver of information pertaining to this amazing character, Petie was again arrested for assault in 1903 and later that year was playing ball in Fortuna, California. His subsequent life and death remain unknown.

4. Based on research by baseball historian Bill Deane, e-mail, November 16, 2002.

5. The October 30, 1886, issue of the *New York Clipper* concurred with the description, according to Deane, saying Dundon had umpired a game in Mobile, Alabama, and "gave entire satisfaction."

6. Reeder, "Old Letter Credits Army Officer," and his February 7, 1970, letter, which is on file at the Baseball Library in Cooperstown. While little supporting material has come to light since the letter was turned over to the Hall of Fame in 1970, it seems to have satisfied former sportswriter Ken Smith, then the director of the Baseball Hall of Fame, who was quoted in *The Sporting News*, calling it a find of "major importance in the manner of an archeological discovery."

7. E-mail citation from Peter Morris, the baseball historian, who happened on this account, was unable to find any indication that the scheme was actually tested on September 9, as planned. One possibility was that President McKinley had been shot two days earlier, so perhaps this signaling idea was dropped. The indoor baseball referred to is the game that, after it moved outside, became softball. This is documented in my *Worth Book of Softball* (New York: Facts on File, 1992), 47–49.

8. The Hoy story seems to have cropped up after his death in 1961 and was never claimed by Hoy himself, nor is it mentioned in any feature article written about Hoy during his lifetime. One interview with Hoy suggests where the story may have begun. Quoting from Bill Deane's posting on SABR-L #29685, March 2001: "In *The Silent Worker*, April 1952, Hoy states that 'the coacher at third kept me posted by lifting his right hand for strikes and his left for balls. This gave later day umpires an idea and they now raise their right . . . to emphasize an indisputable strike.' This indicates that this practice was adopted after Hoy's career; and, as far as we know, Hoy merely assumed that his coaches' signals were the inspiration for this idea."

In an e-mail of November 16, 2002, Deane, who is working on a book on baseball myths, notes the extent of the Hoy myth: "Hoy was the reason umpires developed hand signals for outs, strikes, balls, fouls, et al., according to *Sports Collectors Digest*. 'Umpires began to use hand signals for his benefit in 1886.' *The Sporting News* agrees that Hoy 'was responsible for the system of hand signals universally adopted by umpires.' The book *Baseball by the Rules* states that 'he persuaded the authorities to introduce hand signals.'"

9. Spalding 1909 and McGowen's textbook, *Bill McGowan's School for Umpires*, 5–6.

10. Cobb, "Tricks That Won Me Ball Games," 63.

11. Kerr, "Signal Tipping Scam of 1909," 52–53, 65. In one version of this story it is the *H* in *Highlanders*, and in another it is an *H* that appears in a whiskey ad. But Kevin P. Kerr, who has done the most extensive research on the event and whose work was the prime source for this recounting, says that all the period descriptions, including all of the articles in *Sporting Life* on the incident, says it was the *H* in *Hat*.

12. Goewey, "The Old Fan," 146.

13. The team in question, the Washington Senators, had posted a record of 42-110 in 1909 and would improve to 66-85 by the time the 1910 season ended. Goewey does little to refute the claims but points out that nobody had come forth to claim the rewards offered for proof.

14. In 1908 three teams in both the American and the National Leagues finished within one and a half games of one another, while the pennants were decided on the last day of the season. The trio in the poem: shortstop Joe Tinker, second baseman Johnny "the Crab" Evers, and first baseman–manager Frank Chance: the name of Adams's short poem was "Baseball's Sad Lexicon"—"sad" in that the poet was a Giants fan—and went like this:
    These are the saddest of possible words
    Tinker to Evers to Chance
    A trio of bear Cubs and fleeter than birds
    Tinker to Evers to Chance
    Ruthlessly pricking our gonfalon bubble
    Making a Giant hit into a double
    Words that are weighty with nothing but trouble
    Tinker to Evers to Chance.

15. Years later, in an interview, Merkle described it this way:

When Bridwell shot that long single, I started across the grass for the clubhouse. Matty was near me. When Evers began shouting for the ball, he noticed something was wrong. Matty caught me by the arm and told me to wait a minute. We walked over toward 2B, and Matty spoke to [Bob] Emslie. "How about this, Bob, is there any trouble with the score of the play?" "It's all right," said Emslie. "You've got the game. I don't see anything wrong with the play." Matty then took me by the arm, and we walked to the clubhouse confident that we had won the game.

16. Detroit Tigers, four games to one. The Cubs victory in the Series was a high point for the franchise and, as David Anderson points out in *More than Merkle*, "put the Cubs on a short list of immortals, teams who have won two straight World Series." Other teams have won three or more pennants in a row, but none of those teams won a pennant by a closer margin than the Chicago Cubs. This Cubs team finished second to the Pirates in 1909 and won another pennant in 1910.

3. Psychological Warfare

1. Fullerton, "Watch His Arm!," 465–66.
2. Mathewson, *Pitching in a Pinch*, 140–41.
3. John J. Evers would make this point for years to come, even going as far as denying Kling's guilt in a bylined article for the *New York Times*. Evers, "Stallings Will Show Up Mackmen," 10.
4. Mathewson, *Pitching in a Pinch*, 143.
5. The central tenet of Mack's offensive strategy was simple: if one knew what pitch was coming, the batter had a decided advantage over the pitcher, and this ability could win many ball games. Billy Evans, the Hall of Fame American League umpire, wrote an article for *Pearson's Magazine* about an outfielder named Briscoe Robotham Lord who had a fine eye (netting him the nickname "the Human Eyeball") and a powerful swing, but was unable to hit the curve. He started his career as an A's bench warmer, where he did so badly in the 1907 season that he was sent back to the Minors. He was bought by Cleveland and then was traded back to the A's in 1910 for an option on Joe Jackson. "Just as soon as Lord rejoined the Athletics he began to pick up on his batting," Evans wrote. "Pitchers who used to fool him with their curves found that he stepped into the twister and hit it 'on the nose.' Suggesting that the A's were allegedly putting him wise to each pitch." Evans had no firm evi-

dence that this was so but said, "I do know from my own observations that when Bris Lord was wearing an Athletic uniform he was a far more dangerous hitter than when garbed in a Cleveland outfit." All of which added to Connie Mack's reputation. Evans, "Tipping the Signals," 32–38.

6. Claudy, *Battle of Base-Ball*, 3–13. Though rare, this would not be the last time that a mascot would be accused of such a thing: we will see this theme again later with the case of Bernie Brewer.

7. "Mascot Faust Not Wanted," *New York Times*, January 31, 1912, 9. But Davis is only admitting that half their sign-stealing was a bluff but does not address the issue of the other half. What he is quick to admit, rather gleefully, however, is that the A's "used all sorts of fake signals" to confound the Giants.

8. Christy Mathewson, "Why We Lost Three World's Championships," *Everybody's Magazine*, October 1914, 756–57.

9. Mack, *Connie Mack's Baseball Book*, 174.

10. Goewey, "The Old Fan Says," 254.

11. Fullerton, "Watch His Arm!," 464–65.

12. Fullerton, "Watch His Arm!," 464.

13. Fred Snodgrass on Taylor: "He wanted to be one of us, to be a full-fledged member of the team. If we went to a vaudeville show, he wanted to know what the joke was, and someone had to tell him. So we all learned. We practiced all the time. We'd go by elevated train from the hotel to the Polo Grounds and all during the ride we'd be spelling out the advertising signs. . . . Even today, when I pass a billboard I find myself doing it." Quoted by Ritter in *Glory of Their Times*, 101.

14. "Luther Taylor, 82, Dies," *New York Times*, August 24, 1958, 86. A letter from Stephen Redmond, MD, Morgan Hill CA, was published in the "Dear Abby" newspaper column of November 12, 2002, addressing the issue of disabilities in which it is alleged that Taylor invented baseball signs. His claim:

In the early 1900s, the New York Giants baseball team had a pitcher named Luther H. Taylor. He was a deaf mute who was, in an era of insensitivity, nicknamed "Dummy." Taylor lost a lot of games due to his inability to communicate with his teammates. John McGraw, the manager of the Giants, was under enormous pressure from the team's owner, the fans and the sportswriters to trade Taylor. Instead, McGraw required the entire Giant team to learn American Sign Language. Once that was accomplished, McGraw used hand signals to lead his team. That's the origin of the hand signals that are used in baseball today.

There is not a scintilla of evidence to support the "pressure" to get rid of Taylor or that this was the origin of hand signals.

15. Klem's recollection of the event appears in the article "Umpire Bill Klem's Own Story" in *Collier's*, April 14, 1951. Klem recalls McGraw's actual message to Robinson: "This is my party. Get the hell out of here." A summary of the evening's events also appears in Kavanaugh and Macht, *Uncle Robbie*, 53.

16. Crusinberry, "Secret Factors," 43–47.

17. Bush, "Lost Arts in Baseball," 54–58.

4. Magicians and Mimes

1. Despite the terminology, there has never been any proof that there was a livelier ball introduced into the game, only a fresher ball. The Live Ball Era was more clearly typified by the fact that strategy and talent pointed to the fences. Ruth's amazing 1920 season happened before the fallout from the Chapman incident. With slugging in the ascendance, the notion of a more strategic, carefully signaled offense began to seem old-fashioned and superfluous. "Why not ask Babe—he's an 'orful good feller—what's his sign for a home run?" was the tag line to a routine in *Baseball Magazine* about a ball club that was so dense that its players felt their signs were unstealable because, in the words of one of them, "there wasn't a guy on this ballclub ever understood 'em." Phelon, "New Set of Baseball Signals," 800–802.

2. Smelser, *Life That Ruth Built*, 520–21. "Durocher was hardly the most objective of observers having been released from the Yankees after being accused of stealing from Babe Ruth's wallet in 1929."

3. Hern, "Old Camp Ground Visit," 7.

4. Ossie Vitt in his days as manager of the Cleveland Indians actually called McCarthy the "toughest" man to steal from.

5. When Ruth died in 1948, the story of the "called shot" appeared in almost every newspaper in America, and some even made it the central anecdote of his life. The *Washington DC Evening Star* headlined an eight-paragraph article on the Babe, "Ruth Climaxed Fabulous Career by Calling Shot on Homer in '32," August 17, 1948. The article opened: "As long as baseball is played the memory will live

of a bulbous man on matchstick legs pointing in eloquent gesture to Wrigley Field's faraway centerfield barrier, the jibes of 50,000 Chicago fans searing his ears." Holtzman's article appeared in the *Chicago Tribune*, June 29, 1991.

6. From an undated one-page biographical press release in the Dressen file at the National Baseball Library, from "Cincinnati Baseball Club," by Gene Karst, information director. The release was written in late 1935 or early 1936.

7. These comments appeared in Dressen's September 11, 1966, *New York Times* obituary.

8. Abramson, "Larceny on the Diamond," 20. This story will be repeated again in 1953, when Dressen is manager of the Dodgers and skipper of the National League All-Stars. Dressen would go on to manage in Brooklyn, Washington, Detroit, and Milwaukee and would coach for a number of teams, including the Yankees and Giants—in fact, he held the distinction of being the only man to have been part of three New York championship teams: the Giants in 1933, the Dodgers in 1941, and the Yankees in 1947. He was a brash man who attracted the descriptive "peppery" by sportswriters and was known for his chili, which he cooked in batches for large numbers. Dressen may be the only man ever to have a recipe published in *The Sporting News*. There is a little-known rule in American letters that when chili is mentioned between the covers of a book, one is honor bound to give the recipe, even if it is not up to one's personal standards. Here is Charlie Dressen's "secret" recipe for making chili:

10 pounds onions
2 cans chili powder
2 bunches celery
1 can tomato juice
6 large cans tomatoes
14 large cans kidney beans
14 pounds chopped meat
1 can dried peppers (hot)
10 tablespoons fat

1. Dice onions and celery. Chop contents of six cans of tomatoes very fine. Place onions, celery, and tomatoes in pot with four quarts of water, and boil for 90 minutes.

2. Brown chopped meat in fat. Add two cans chili powder.

3. Mix chopped meat into pot. Add one can tomato juice, plus
one can of water.
4. Cook over medium flame and spoon off fat (but leave enough
fat for flavor).
5. Add hot peppers and salt to taste.
Serves 160 people.
9. Greenberg, *Hank Greenberg*, 138. As hard as it seems to believe today,
the two men were in Greenberg's account actually pointing the rifle,
albeit unloaded, in the direction of home plate. In Aviva Kempner's
film *The Life and Times of Hank Greenberg*, Greenberg is shown
saying that the central reason for the Tigers' success in 1940 was the
fact that they were stealing signs. Baker would continue to perform
his magic for many years to come, spending a total of twenty-eight
years in the Tigers organization, as well as performing managerial
and coaching stints in Boston and Cleveland, but he did so with a
remarkable ability to play the innocent. In 1944 Ed Rumill of *Baseball
Magazine* asked him about his oft-mentioned abilities, and he denied
ever having stolen a single sign. "It's the bunk" is how he put it.
10. L. Smith of the *Detroit Free Press*, "Signing Off," 54. For years to
come, this Series was used to underscore the fact that there are
limitations to the value of a stolen sign. The Tigers were able to call
every pitch that Derringer threw for the Reds in the sixth game, but
they were still shut out 4–0. Wish Egan, a former member of the
Tiger organization, later revealed to Smith: "To this day, I can't figure out how we lost, but the record books say we did."
11. Tebbetts, "I'd Rather Catch," 45. This article is posted on the website
of the *Atlantic Monthly*.
12. James, *Bill James Guide*, 185–87.
13. Schneider, *Boys of the Summer*, 38–42.
14. Schneider, *Boys of the Summer*, 38–42. In 1948, when many in the
American League maintained that the Indians were stealing signs
from the scoreboard, Boudreau scoffed at the charges. His public assessment of the 1948 season was that that was the year he had
"angels on shoulders." But when his tenure with the Indians was
over in 1950, he admitted to Arthur Daley of the *New York Times*
that telescopic intervention had been tried "a few times." Bill Veeck,
owner of the team, later discharged the incident as nothing more
than part of Cleveland's "long tradition of scoreboard espionage,"
although he had originally denied all.

During mid-August 1949 the Red Sox manager became so convinced that the Cleveland scoreboard housed a utility infielder with a telescope that he got an umpiring crew to decree that all apertures in said scoreboard had to be sealed shut. This was soon forgotten, and by 1954 Ed McAuley of the *Cleveland News* reported in an article in *Baseball Digest*, "This year, the doors at either end of the board are wide open and a block in the middle of the board has been taken out to provide better ventilation."

Seven years after the navy telescope incident, there would be another case involving military hardware in which Boudreau was the victim. In May 1955 Boudreau was the new manager of the Kansas City Athletics and, convinced that his catcher's signs were being stolen, sent one of his coaches out to look for a peephole in the scoreboard. He discovered that the army had innocently displayed some of its tanks, trucks, and jeeps behind a low fence in center field as part of a recruiting drive. Standing next to a jeep was a telescope mounted on a tripod, which was all that Boudreau needed to conclude that one of the Cleveland relief pitchers stationed himself by the telescope and transmitted the Kansas City signs to reliever Hal Newhouser, who was sprawled out on the bench in the bullpen. When the future Hall of Famer spread his legs, it meant a fastball was about to be pitched. When he crossed his legs, a curve was coming. As second baseman Spooks Jacobs recalled, "That telescope was so powerful that you could see the white on the fingernails of the catcher." Hank Greenberg, Indians general manager, called these charges "preposterous"—presumably with a smile on his face, as he had not revealed what had transpired in the 1940 pennant drive. Boudreau, it seems, did protest too much. By the end of the season there were widespread accusations that Boudreau was using a surveyor's telescope, which he had positioned in his bullpen. In the postseason Boudreau denied the allegation—but not, to use Arthur Daley's term, "vigorously." From Daley's November 17, 1955, *New York Times* column: "'It is not true,' he said and then timidly added, 'to my knowledge.'"

15. Bob Considine, "Mister Mack," *Saturday Evening Post*, 93–95, 100–102, undated clippings.
16. King, "Zany Antics Flash Help Sign."
17. Muskat, *Banks to Sandberg to Grace*, 8, of an excerpt of this book at baseballlibrary.com.

5. Cheaters, Stealers, and Scoreboard Spies

1. *The Sporting News*, "Too Many Signals Burden Batters," 16. Cobb had certain managers in mind, such as Al Lopez, Cleveland skipper in the 1950s, who made a name for himself directing every element of his team's game, save for calling the pitches. In general, teams were being run this way, and the autonomy of many batters was disappearing.

2. Veeck, *Veeck—as in Wreck*, 159.

3. Three summers later, perhaps angered that the Dodgers had not renewed his contract and that he was relegated to managing the last-place Washington Senators, Dressen declared, "In 1952, when I managed the Dodgers, I stole enough signs to win us nine games. That year, Brooklyn won the pennant by only four and a half."

4. Abramson, "Larceny on the Diamond," 50; J. Lardner, "Spies and Hangovers," 88.

5. J. Lardner, "Spies and Hangovers," 88.

6. "Although this sounds like pure Yogi-speak, it is a system that was employed by more than one battery. It was as simple as adding any given number on the scoreboard—say, the total number of errors—to the finger sign to get an odd or even number: the odd number for the fastball and the even number for the breaking ball.

7. Einstein, *Fireside Book of Baseball*, 72.

8. Louis Effrat, "Larsen Says His No Wind-Up Delivery Aided Control and Kept Batters Tense," *New York Times*, October 9, 1956, 50. Others copied Larsen. For instance, manager Harry Craft of the Kansas City Athletics was convinced that his pitchers were having their pitches called by telltale mannerisms during 1956, so for 1957, his first year as manager, he instituted a new system of standardized delivery without elaborate windups and stretches and a procedure for hiding the ball as it was being fingered prior to delivery.

9. Muskat, *Banks to Sandberg to Grace*, 8, of an excerpt of this book at baseballlibrary.com.

10. *Sports Illustrated*, "Signals and Spies," 44. The initial report of the Richards protest is in the *New York Times* on June 23, 1956, in an article titled "Mantle Draws Walk."

11. *Sports Illustrated*, "Signs and Science," 28; Effrat, "Special Lens for Baseball TV," 33; Drebinger, "TV Fans See Catcher's Signals," 31.

12. Veeck, *Veeck—as in Wreck*, 162–63.

13. "Shooting Scoreboard Strafes Chicago Infield," *New York Times*, June 5, 1960, S3.
14. Veeck, *Veeck—as in Wreck*, 161.
15. *The Sporting News*, "Conlan Tells Brave Bull-Pen," 25.
16. Don Zimmer, interview by the author, Tampa FL, Yankees Royals exhibition game, March 15, 2002. Zimmer added that they were picking signs from Cubs catcher Elvin Tappe's signs and telegraphing their findings via a crude scoreboard semaphore. See also *Sports Illustrated*, "Spy Story"; and *The Sporting News*, "Say It Ain't So, Cholly," 14.
17. Munzel, "Tepee 'Cub Scouts,'" 21.
18. Burnes, "Sign-Stealing by Remote Control?," 88–93. The article originally appeared in the *St. Louis Globe-Democrat*.
19. "Braves Protest 6–2 Loss to Cubs," *New York Times*, September 5, 1961, 45. The protest went nowhere, and the umpiring crew did not order the slots closed.
20. Hornsby and Surface, "You've Got to Cheat to Win," 59–62, 101–3.

6. Revisionist Finger-Pointers

1. Broeg, "Giants Stole Signals," 15; Daniel, "Daniel Traces Signal-Swiping History," 15. National League secretary Fred Fleig told Bob Broeg after the winter meetings, "I think the greatest complaint came from Birdie Tebbetts about alleged spying out of the scoreboard in Chicago." Tebbetts, the Braves' manager, had played a September 4, 1961, game against the Cubs under protest and clearly wanted baseball's authorities to deal with the issue.
2. Hornsby and Surface, *My War with Baseball*. Stengel struggled to say anything good about Hornsby. The last lines of the foreword were the most positive: "He said what he thought. He lost a lot of managing jobs. He had a number of arguments—public and private. But he never backed up from anybody on the baseball field or in the front office." In Florida in 1962 he had become so angry that he ranted over such trivialities as men wearing Bermuda shorts. Hornsby died on January 5 of the next year, and his hatred of flowers appeared in death notices as "No flowers."
3. For instance, Hornsby proudly told of an event that took place after being hired for three years as manager of the St. Louis Browns by Bill Veeck. This took place during the spring of 1952, following the incident in which Bill Veeck had brought three-foot-seven Eddie Gaedel

into the game as a publicity stunt and after Hornsby had told Veeck
that he would not abide any new publicity stunts. Quoting directly:
We opened spring training in El Centro, California, and about
the first thing I saw was two carloads of those little old midgets
driving up and running out on the field where we were trying to
get in shape to play major league baseball. My message was simple and loud: "Get the hell out of here and don't come back. We
don't want that kind of stuff around here." One of those little old
midgets just stared at me. So I picked him up by the seat of the
pants and collar and threw him over the railing. I wasn't going to
put up with that nonsense.

4. "Maris in Row with Hornsby," *Baltimore Sun*, March 23, 1962, Sports
section, 1–2.

5. "Most Big Clubs Steal Signs—Hornsby," *Cincinnati Inquirer*, March
25, 1962, H3.

6. The UPI story is unsigned and variously titled. It appears in the
Philadelphia Inquirer, for example, under the title "Hook Says Reds
Stole Catchers' Signs" on March 21, 1962, Sports section, 3. Law-
rence's denial appears in an AP story with various titles such as
"Deny Sign-Stealing," *Los Angeles Herald Examiner*, March 21, 1963,
Sports section, 2.

7. Schecter's report was selected for the anthology *The Best Sport Stories of 1963*, 55–57.

8. The earliest published reference to sign-stealing in the 1951 playoffs
was a detailed sixteen-paragraph wire-service story by Joe Reichler,
the highly respected Associated Press writer with a March 22, 1962,
Fort Lauderdale FL dateline. "Spy Aided Thomson's Dramatic '51
Homer," *Los Angeles Times*, March 23, 1962, Sports section, 1; "Did
Giants Steal Signs? 1959 Scoreboard 'Spying' Claimed," *San Francisco
Chronicle*, March 23, 1962, 39.

9. "Thomson Denies Secret Signal Led to Pennant-Winning Homer,"
New York Times, March 24, 1962, 19. The *New York Daily News* ran
the second-day lead with Thomson's rebuttal under the headline
"Bobby Says, 'Ridiculous.'" Both the Dodgers and the Giants had
moved west in 1958, and the story died quickly in New York but was
big news elsewhere, especially in San Francisco and Los Angeles.

10. "Indignant Giants Berate Source of 'Spy' Charges," *Atlanta Constitution*,
March 24, 1962, Sports section, 3; "Thomson Homer Not on 'Steal,' Says
Branca," *Los Angeles Times*, March 24, 1962, Sports section, 3.

11. "Stolen Sign Tale Denied," *San Francisco Chronicle*, March 24, 1962, 31–32.
12. Bob Hunter, "Lippy Denies Stealing Signs," *Los Angeles Herald Examiner*, March 23, 1962, C4.
13. McDonald, "Signal Stealing," 10. I showed Retrosheet's David W. Smith this column, and he reacted to the assertion that Thomson missed it "by a good foot" on the first pitch: "However, there is no doubt at all that he took that pitch!" McDonald was wrong. The first pitch was a called pitch.
14. Despite respectable numbers, Worthington was demoted to the Minors by the White Sox and did not get another shot until 1963. He played the 1962 season for the Indianapolis Indians, a White Sox farm club in the American Association. In 1962 the White Sox spring training camp was in Sarasota, giving him a reason to be in South Florida for the interview. But there is no evidence to suggest that he actually got a chance with the Sox. National Baseball Library researcher Bill Francis reported in answer to a query on Worthington's location: "He wasn't on the spring training roster," and none of the spring training notes from *The Sporting News* mentioned him. In an article dated November 27, 1962, after he was signed by the Mets, Al Lopez said, "We could have used Worthington ourselves the last two years. But we couldn't bring back a player who had quit on us." He was acquired by the New York Mets at the end of the Indianapolis season, where he had posted a 15-4 record and a 2.94 earned run average. Ironically, Rogers Hornsby, the man who had mocked him for his honesty and distaste for cheating, was the one who spotted him for the Mets. The Mets were desperate for pitching, and Hornsby's comment that Worthington was "the best" Minor League pitcher he had seen appears in an article in the *New York Times* of September 28, 1962, by Louis Effrat, titled "Only 595 See Mets Lose 119th as Also-Forlorn Cubs Win 3–2," 25. Worthington, a born-again Christian, coached baseball for Jerry Falwell's Liberty College and still makes appearances at baseball clinics and dinners.

Remarkably, a search of all the major newspapers suggests that no one asked Dressen about the matter. Dressen, who would die in 1966, was between managerial jobs. His last year with the Braves was 1961, and his first with Detroit was 1963. Many papers did not follow up on the story, and McDonald was one of the few big-name columnists to comment on it. Others stayed away in droves, including Red

Smith of the *New York Herald Tribune,* John Daley of the *New York Times,* Shirley Povich of the *Washington Post,* and Morrie Siegel of the *Washington DC Daily News.* The much more interesting topic for the era's sports pundits was the ongoing turmoil surrounding Roger Maris, who had broken Babe Ruth's record the year before and who was by all accounts as angry with the press as they were with him. "Whatever is eating at Roger has a gluttonous appetite," wrote Francis Stann of the *Washington DC Evening Star*—in which he takes a number of pokes at him, including calling him "the asterisk home run king."

15. Allen Lewis, "Ex-Spy Mauch Laughs at Sign Furor," *Philadelphia Inquirer,* March 24, 1962, 16.

16. See note 1.

17. Worthington, who had become a mediocre starter, came back to play for Cincinnati in 1963 and went to the Twins in 1964, where he became one of the American League's best, saving twenty-one games in 1965 and leading the American League in saves with eighteen in 1968, the year before saves became an official statistic.

18. Piersall, "How the Home Team Cheats," 21–23, 61–62.

19. Veeck, *Veeck—as in Wreck,* 162.

20. Daley, "Grand Larceny," June 25, 1962, 32.

21. Newhan, "Some of Baseball's Best Thieves," C7.

22. Making this even more complex was the fact that the nature of pitching was changing, and the assortment of pitches seemed to be growing. Retired catcher Joe Garagiola, writing as a Yankee broadcaster for the *1966 Baseball Guidebook,* theorized, "Old-time pitchers usually had three serves—a fastball, curve and change-up—but young players who have come out of the Little Leagues, Babe Ruth Leagues, American Legion, etc. have six or seven different pitches and throw them with two or three different motions." The result was that a catcher had to have signs for as many as eight pitches— fastball, curve, changeup, knuckleball, screwball, palm ball, sinker, and slider—not including an occasional trick pitch.

7. Big Tippers

1. Lebovitz, "'Built-In Radar,'" 10; "A Disabled Turley Still Valuable Asset," *Los Angeles Times,* March 13, 1988, Sports section, 3. It would also be the last time any person was charged publicly with stealing signs from outside the playing field in American baseball.

Among other things, they had also become a victim of technology. From this point forward, whatever skullduggery was performed was done with the aid of center-field television cameras, which can pick up a catcher's signs, while other cameras can record a third base coach's signals.

2. Will, *Men at Work.* Pitchers were widely read, and the newspapers often pointed them out as a public service: Jay Hook, the man who had told on the Reds, showed his fingering during the spring of 1963 for the Mets to the point where reporters could tell what he was about to throw, and the Mets' Roger Craig was ordered to mask his grip after giving up easy clues to his next pitch. Craig went out to post a 10-24 win-loss record for the nascent 1962 Mets (5-22 for 1963), so his grip may have been embedded in a larger number of problems, including a team that would end its freshman year with a 40-120 record. Occasionally, a pitcher would discover the tip himself. A case in point was Cletis Boyer of the Yankees, who told a reporter that *he* was tipping the pitchers in the American League when he was getting ready to tag a fastball by digging in his heels and leaning forward, and once he discovered this he came out of a slump. Boyer was inviting the pitcher to toss a curve or come inside.

3. Daley, "Grand Larceny," June 25, 1962, 32; interview with Roger Angell, spring training, Tampa FL, March 2001. Some players loved getting tipped signs, while others refused, or at least claimed to have no interest in stolen signs. "I wouldn't take a sign if their own catcher sent it to me Western Union," Yogi Berra once announced. Hank Aaron, Eddie Mathews, Tony Gwynn, Cal Ripken Jr., and Reggie Jackson are among those who have let it be known that they did not want to be given the nature of the next pitch. "I never took signs. I didn't want them. I didn't need them," said Jackson in a 2001 interview. A few players seemed to have special abilities that transcended the issue. "Wade Boggs didn't need to know, but he knew everything about the pitcher—looks at how he puts ball in glove, could even pick up the spin on the ball," said Billy Hatcher when he was coaching with Boggs for Tampa Bay in 2001.

4. *Sports Illustrated*, "I Spy," 11.

5. The issue went no further, and the scouts stayed in the press box.

6. UPI, "Robinson Accuses White Sox of Cheating," April 25, 1991.

7. Lebovitz, "Indians Best Kept Secret," B2. At the beginning of his twelfth consecutive season as bench coach for the White Sox, the

team's 2002 *Media Guide* was still able to boast of Nossek that he was "reputed to be a master at stealing signs" (29).

8. Kurkjian, "Sign Language," 62.
9. McCue, "Baseball's Sign Language," H9.
10. Newhan, "Some of Baseball's Best Thieves." In an interview with the *Los Angeles Times,* Mauch also said, "I hit .350 in the Pacific Coast League one year; if I couldn't have read signs, I couldn't have hit .350 in batting practice."
11. Kurkjian, "Sign Language," 63.
12. "Bad Blood Boiling between Alou, Baker," *Austin (TX) American-Statesman,* May 10, 1997, E5. The concept of stealing—signs or bases—with a large lead is always controversial: "I can remember Casey Stengel saying at one time when he had a lead of nine or ten runs that he still stole bases. People got mad with him," said Syd Thrift, Baltimore Orioles vice president for baseball operations. "Stengel said if you can guarantee me that you won't score more runs than this, I'll stop running." "When I was a young player with the Dodgers and Maury Wills was so effective," remembered Jeff Torberg, "we needed every run we could get." That said, it is still dangerous to do something that appears to rub salt in the defensive team's collective wounds. Thrift and Torberg were interviewed by the author in spring training of 2002.
13. Tom Keegan, "Bobby V: I'm Not a Crook," *New York Post,* from a Bobby Valentine collection of articles, "Bobby? Troublemaker? Perhaps," from an unpaginated collection of articles on Valentine on the *Post* website. This was also the visit during which a horticultural issue was raised concerning a patch of sunflowers and corn and tomato plants that rose high in the New York Mets' bullpen. The height of the plants prevented opposing teams from seeing into the bullpen. Philly manager Terry Francona mentioned this to umpire Frank Pulli and asked that someone keep him informed of who was warming up. Mets manager Bobby Valentine denied "devious planting," and Francona denied cutting the cable. "Valentine admittedly enjoyed the paranoia the camera story created," said the *New York Post*'s Tom Keegan, adding, "Valentine also pointed out that many other teams have video cameras in suspicious locales."
14. Interview with the author. During the same discussion George Brett, Royals vice president for baseball operations, smiles when asked

about the state of the art of stealing from second base and says, "There's sure a lot of that going on these days."

15. Boswell, "Some Players Peek Early." See also White, "Why Is Peeking Such a Sin?," 2.

16. Hernandez and Bryan, *Pure Baseball*, 127. He also admits, "I peeked myself, now and then, not too often."

17. Dixon, "Sign-Stealing Flap"; Yuri Kageyama, "Japan Scandal: Sign-Stealing Scam Has Officials Investigating Sadaharu Oh," *Detroit News*, December 4, 1998; Japan Times Online, "Buffaloes' GM Suspended by PL in Sign-Stealing Case," June 23, 2001.

18. The stories of the dumb player who could not get the sign was usually set in the past or told apocryphally. The most often told example from the 1960s took place when Frank Howard was with the Dodgers and the use of a player's last name signaled a hit-and-run play. Once after the big man walked, he began hearing chatter from his first base coach, Pete Reiser: "Stay alive, Howard." The pitch was thrown and he didn't run, so Reiser shouted even louder, "Stay alive! Howard!" The slugger called Reiser to the bag and whispered, "We've been friends all these years—and I call you Pete. Why have you suddenly stopped calling me Frank?"

19. Certain clubs were fortunate in having an older pro who could take hold of a pitcher, show him his flaws, and help him to make adjustments. A good example of this took place in mid-1998, when the expansion Tampa Bay Devil Rays pitcher Rolando Arrojo went into a midseason slump and then came out of it, becoming the first pitcher on an expansion team to reach fourteen victories. "The main thing was Wade Boggs. He told me I was tipping my pitches," Arrojo told the *St. Petersburg (FL) Times.*

8. Epitaph for a Miracle

1. Mushnick, "Branca, Thomson Still in There Singin'," 3. Phil Mushnick of the *New York Post* reported that a video of this moment was played on January 2001 at a charity dinner in New York, at which point Thomson and Branca reprised their duet.

2. Jane Gross, "Thomson Homer Wears Well," *New York Times*, July 21, 1982, B7.

3. Devaney, "Baseball's Secret Sign Language," 22.

4. *The Game and the Glory* (1976) and *Baseball's Great Moments* (1974) are two examples. In both there is no question that his reverence for

the miracle is fully intact, and it was certainly not because he was timid. An article he wrote on segregated facilities in Florida spring training in the late 1950s made him unpopular among the locals, who on one occasion booed and hissed at a meeting of local citizens in St. Petersburg. His son Peter recalled in his father's obituary in *Newsday*, "In response all the black ballplayers on the dais stood up . . . and started applauding. And the rest of the ballplayers stood up and began applauding." Fresco, "Joseph Reichler," 35.

5. Thomson, *Giants Win the Pennant!*, 177–79.

6. Prager, "Was the '51 Giants Comeback a Miracle?"

7. Boswell, "Miracle of Coogan's Bluff Tarnished," D1.

8. Waldstein, "Giants Won the Pennant."

9. A *New York Daily News* story by Vic Ziegel suggested the story be put to rest: "The reporter asked Thomson if he took the sign. Asked him more than once. 'My answer is no,' Thomson said. Good answer. End of story. Go away. Leave us alone." Ziegel, "About Time We Gave This Story a Rest," 78.

10. Miller and Connor, "Old-Timers Admit They Cheated," 3.

11. Kiernan, *Miracle at Coogan's Bluff*, 102, and his letter to the *New York Times*, October 14, 2001. Kiernan, the author of a 1975 book on the subject, *The Miracle of Coogan's Bluff*, described his interview with Walker for his book in the wake of the *Wall Street Journal* article. Kiernan also insisted that the scheme was not only the talk of the Dodgers' clubhouse in the last few months of the '51 season but also scoffed at as just another "Durocher ploy" designed to rattle opposing teams. One of his sources for this was Branca.

12. Stout, *Yankees Century*.

13. D. Smith, "Play by Play Analysis."

Batting and pitching data for 1951 Giants before and after July 20

BATTING	Before July 20		After July 19	
	G	BA	G	BA
At home	48	.263	30	.256
On road	40	.252	39	.269

PITCHING	Before July 20			After July 19		
	W	L	ERA	W	L	ERA
At home	26	22	3.44	24	6	2.80
On road	21	19	4.53	27	12	3.00

These numbers come from a letter of June 19, 2001, from David W. Smith, in which he reiterated that the Giants batters "actually did WORSE at home after July 19 while improving a lot on the road."

14. D. Smith, "Play by Play Analysis."

15. Kleinberg, contacted for this book, had never heard of the 1962 revelations but was not surprised. He just couldn't see why it was a story in 2001, or, as he put it, "In an exchange of E-mails I had with the *Wall Street Journal* writer, he questioned whether I was trying to say he stole the material, I assured him I was not questioning that, just wondering what makes the story of the signal stealing—reported in print at least 10 years ago—so significant today."

16. An extensive search by various members of the staff at the National Baseball Library and a detailed search of the *New York Times* and *The Sporting News* and *Baseball Digest*, among others, for 1961–62 yields nothing about a rule change. Koppett, *New Thinking Man's Guide.*

17. The show debuted on July 11, 2001. Among the fascinating details in the HBO documentary was the fact that the nation's largest city left about 20,000 seats empty for the most famous game ever played, adding, "Among the 34,320 who were at the Polo Grounds on that October afternoon was FBI director J. Edgar Hoover, who did not unearth the Giants sign-stealing scheme while sitting with Jackie Gleason and Frank Sinatra." HBO president Ross Greenberg told a reporter that he did not believe Bobby Thomson received a stolen sign when his home run beat Brooklyn. "I believe the Giants shut down the sign-stealing during the three-game play-off," he said. "How else do you explain them losing 10–1 in the Polo Grounds?" In the documentary Branca said, "I think he had the sign," contradicting his comments in 1962. Thomson said it was laughable.

18. Prager, *Echoing Green*, 351.

9. From the TV Camera to the Apple Watch

1. Dave Brady, "Leo Steals Show with Signal-Swiping on TV," *The Sporting News*, May 22, 1965.

2. Murray Chass, "Baseball: League Presidents Out as Baseball Centralizes," *New York Times*, September 16, 1999.

3. Taylor Soper, "Smartphones in the Dugout: T-Mobile Inks Landmark Deal with Major League Baseball," Geekwire, January 9, 2013, https://www.geekwire.com/2013/mlb-tmobile-baseball-dugout-galaxy-samsung/.

4. youtube.com/watch?v=3ero-V9710.

5. In September 2016 when the retiring Ortiz made his farewell tour of baseball, the Orioles presented him with the smashed phone mounted on a stand as a trophy.

6. Robert Patrick, "Another Delay in Sentencing Former St. Louis Cardinals Exec," *St. Louis Post-Dispatch*, May 21, 2016, A5.

7. In a major upset for Apple's smartwatch brand, it appears that it was a Fitbit, not an Apple Watch, that the Red Sox used as a medium for their sign-stealing in a recent ball game. The news comes from "a Major League source" speaking to *Boston Globe* sports reporter Nick Cafardo. It's unclear at this time whether the source himself or herself is Major League or if they are MLB related. Devin Coldewey, *TechCrunch* (New York: AOL, 2017).

8. The full press release of September 15, 2017, "Commissioner's Statement Regarding Red Sox–Yankees Violations," is available at https://www.mlb.com/news/c-254435818.

9. The Goodman article appears on Slate: http://www.slate.com/articles/sports/sports_nut/2017/09/the_red_sox_s_sign_stealing_scheme_was_less_nefarious_than_stupid.html. See also Jim Souhan, "A Right and Wrong Way to Steal," *Minneapolis Star-Tribune*, September 10, 2017, C4.

10. Bob Nightengale, "MLB Must Fix Its September Baseball Problem," *USA Today*, September 7, 2017.

11. Tyler Kepner, "Commissioner Puts Limit on Visits to the Mound," *New York Times*, February 20, 2018, B18.

12. https://www.therapidian.org/october-16–2017-ethics-and-religion-talk-stealing-signs-baseball-unethical.

13. Chris Chavez, "What Does It Mean to Steal Signs in Baseball?," *Sports Illustrated*, September 15, 2007, https://www.si.com/mlb/2017/09/05/sign-stealing-baseball-history.

14. Mark Gonzales, "Cubs Manager Joe Maddon Admits to Sign-Stealing during Coaching Days," TCA *Regional News*, February 20, 2009.

15. https://www.nytimes.com/2017/09/27/sports/baseball/yankees-fan-sign-stealing-ejected.html?partner=bloomberg.

16. E-mail to the author, May 21, 2018.

17. Reiter, *Astroball*, 161.

18. David Waldstein, "For Royals, Outbursts Follow Uproar," *New York Times*, October 21, 2015, B11.

19. Tyler Kepner, "In This Era, Teams Believe They Can't Be Paranoid Enough," *New York Times*, October 18, 2018, B-10 (L).

20. MLB statement on sign-stealing concerns, October 17, 2018, https://www.mlb.com/news/mlb-statement-on-sign-stealing-concerns/c-298051578.

21. Chris Mason, "Sign-Stealing Sideshow Casts Ugly Shadow on ALCS, and It's All the League's Fault," *Newburyport (MA) News*, October 18, 2018.

22. David Sheinin, "Astros–Red Sox Sign-Stealing Flap Puts a Spotlight on Baseball's Technology Problem," *Washington Post*, October 17, 2018, https://www.washingtonpost.com/sports/astros-red-sox-sign-stealing-flap-puts-a-spotlight-on-baseballs-technology-problem/2018/10/17/d79819fe-d256-11e8-b2d2-f397227b43f0_story.html?utm_term=.91efbac431fa.

23. Hayden Bird, "Alex Cora Explained How the Red Sox Exploited the Astros' 'Paranoia,'" October 20, 2018, boston.com/sports/boston-red-sox/2018/10/20/alex-cora-sign-stealing-astros.

24. Mario Porto interview, June 28, 2018, Bethesda MD.

Conclusion

1. Joe Morgan's comment appeared as a special feature on ESPN.com on May 8, 2002, titled "What to Watch? Start with the Catcher." For those who enjoy Morgan's commentary, this essay is loaded with insights like this one: "While a team must defense a superstar out of a game in basketball, football, or hockey, a great baseball player can be taken out of the game completely. It's one of baseball's weaknesses and one of the reasons I believe baseball has drawn fewer fans and viewers."

2. Barber, "How to Watch a Ball Game," 21.

3. Joe DiMaggio, "How to Watch the World Series," *Baltimore Sun*, September 23, 1956, WM12.

4. Gammons, "Sign Language," 7.

5. Goddard, "Third Base Coaches," 40–43.

6. Mack, *Connie Mack's Baseball Book*, 174–75.

7. Joe Sexton, "Big Brother Isn't Watching, but Foote Is," *New York Times*, March 28, 1993, Sports section, G3.

8. Nightingale, "Concentration Is Key to Code-Breaking," 14.

9. Lou Chapman, "Signs by Third Base Coach Show Something's Afoot," *Baseball Digest*, September 1975, 84.

BIBLIOGRAPHY

"You can look it up," he'll say to doubters. They do and doubt no longer.
—REFERENCE TO CASEY STENGEL, *New York Times*, October 19, 1960

Abramson, Martin. "Larceny on the Diamond." *American Weekly*, June 5, 1955.

Addie, Bob. "Sign-Snitching Yarns Stitch Grin Pattern for Dressen." *The Sporting News*, April 6, 1955.

Alexander, Charles C. *John McGraw*. New York: Viking, 1988.

Alston, Walter, and Don Weiskopf. *The Complete Baseball Handbook*. Boston: Allyn and Bacon, 1972.

Amdur, Neil. "Twins Detecting Faults on TV Tape." *New York Times*, May 27, 1968.

Amore, Dom. "In Truth, '51 Team Still Together." *Hartford (CT) Courant*, February 5, 2001.

Anderson, Dave. "Branca Knew '51 Giants Stole Signs." *New York Times*, February 1, 2001.

———. "A Fastball, a Swing and Forever." *New York Times*, October 1, 2001.

Anderson, David. *More than Merkle: A History of the Best and Most Exciting Baseball Season in Human History*. Lincoln: University of Nebraska Press, 2000.

Associated Press. "Giants Players Admit They Stole Signs on Way to 1951 Pennant." February 1, 2001.

———. "Max Patkin, 79, 'Clown Prince of Baseball.'" October 2, 1999.

Bakalar, Nick. *The Baseball Fan's Companion*. New York: Macmillan, 1996.

Bancroft, Jessie H., and William Dean Pulvermacher. *Handbook of Athletic Games*. New York: Macmillan, 1917.

Barber, Red. "How to Watch a Ball Game." *Baseball Digest*, n.d.

Baxter, Kevin. "Simple Gestures Mean So Much in Baseball." *Los Angeles Times*, July 1, 2013.

Beaton, Rod. "Craig Teaches and Learns: His Giants Make the Grade." *USA Today*, October 3, 1989.

Beaton, Rod, and Hal Bodley. "Sign Stealing Isn't New, Most Teams Just Don't Bother to Try." *USA Today*, February 2, 2001.

Bench, Johnny. *The Complete Idiot's Guide to Baseball*. New York: Alpha Books, 1999.

Berg, Moe. "Pitchers and Catchers." *Atlantic Monthly*, September 1941.

Blake, Mike. *Baseball Chronicles*. Cincinnati: Betterway Books, 1994.

Borges, Ron. "Wilson Steals Scene." *Boston Globe*, May 11, 1988.

Boswell, Thomas. "The Miracle of Coogan's Bluff Tarnished." *Washington Post*, February 1, 2001.

———. "Some Players Peek Early, and Some Never Do." *Washington Post*, May 16, 2002.

Brandt, William. "Baseball Signs and Signals." *Baseball Magazine*, July 1931.

Broeg, Bob. "Giants Stole Signals, but Not with Buzzer." *The Sporting News*, April 4, 1962.

———. *Signals: The Secret Language of Baseball in Fingertip Movies*. Boston: Gillette, 1957.

Brosnan, Jim. *The Long Season*. New York: Harper and Row, 1960.

———. *Pennant Race*. New York: Harper and Brothers, 1962.

Brown, Tim. "Reds Point to Smith in Sign-Stealing Flap." *USA Today*, May 7, 1997.

———. "Stealing Signals Sign of Times." *Cincinnati Enquirer*, May 26, 1997.

Burnes, Robert L. "Crime-Doesn't-Pay Dept." *Baseball Digest*, March 1965.

———. "Sign-Stealing by Remote Control? It's Overrated!" *Baseball Digest*, November–December 1960.

Bush, "Bullet Joe." "The Lost Arts in Baseball." *Saturday Evening Post*, April 5, 1930.

Camp, Walter. "Brainwork on the Diamond." *Collier's*, August 2, 1924.

Chicago Daily News. "One Sign Enough." *Baseball Digest*, September 1943.

Cincinnati Enquirer. "How to Foil Sign-Tippers." *Baseball Digest*, September 1950.

Claudy, Carl H. *The Battle of Base-Ball*. New York: Century, 1912.

———. "Signals and Signal-Stealing." *Saint Nicholas Magazine*, June 1913, 714–18.

Cobb, Ty. "Tricks That Won Me Ball Games." *Life*, March 24, 1962.

Cobb, Ty, with Al Stump. *My Life in Baseball: The True Record.* New York: Doubleday, 1961.

Cobbledick, Gordon. "Sure Cure for Sign Stealers." *Baseball Digest,* July 1955.

Cochrane, Gordon S. *Baseball: The Fan's Game.* New York: Funk and Wagnalls, 1939.

Coffin, Tristram Potter. *The Old Ball Game: Baseball in Folklore and Fiction.* New York: Herder and Herder, 1971.

Cohen, Leonard. "High-Way to Unhappiness." *Baseball Digest,* May 1957.

Cole, Jim. "He Needed an Interpreter." *Baseball Digest,* February 1944.

Conlin, Bill. "Bristol Uses a Sign Language All His Own." *The Sporting News,* September 9, 1972.

Cope, Myron. "The Whip Who Put the Snap in the Phillies." *Saturday Evening Post,* August 14, 1964.

Cronin, Joe. "Inside Baseball: Managers Direct Clubs with Sign Language." *San Francisco News,* July 22, 1940.

Crusinberry, James. "Secret Factors in the Winning of a World's Championship." *Baseball Magazine,* April 1914.

Curran, William. *Strikeout.* New York: Crown, 1995.

Daley, Arthur. "Cloak and Dagger Stuff." *New York Times,* November 17, 1955.

———. "Confessions of a Sign-Stealer." *Baseball Digest,* September, 1943.

———. "Grand Larceny." *New York Times,* August 17, 1950.

———. "Grand Larceny." *New York Times,* June 25, 1962.

———. "Thinking Made Easy." *New York Times,* August 21, 1967.

Daniel, Dan. "Daniel Traces Signal-Swiping History to '76." *The Sporting News,* April 4, 1962.

Davidson, Gary. "Book Closed on Pitch-Tipping Case—or Is It?" *The Sporting News,* March 13, 1982.

———. "Minors Probe 'Tipping' Charges." *The Sporting News,* September 12, 1981.

Deindorfer, Bob. "Baseball's Counter-spies." In *The Fireside Book of Baseball,* edited by Charles Einstein. New York: Simon and Schuster, 1958.

———. "Secrets of the Sign Stealers." *Baseball Digest,* October 1953, 43–50.

Delmonico, Rod. *Hit and Run Baseball.* Champaign IL: Leisure Press, 1992.

Devaney, John. "Baseball's Secret Sign Language." *American Legion Magazine,* June 1968.

Dickson, Paul. *Bill Veeck: Baseball's Greatest Maverick.* New York: Walker, 2012.

———. *The Dickson Baseball Dictionary*. Edited by Skip McAfee. 3rd ed. New York: W. W. Norton, 2009.

———. *Leo Durocher: Baseball's Prodigal Son*. New York: Bloomsbury, 2017.

———. *The New Dickson Baseball Dictionary*. San Diego: Harcourt, Brace, 1999.

Dittmar, Joe. "A Shocking Discovery." *Baseball Research Journal* 20 (1991).

Dixon, Oscar. "Sign-Stealing Flap Hits Japan Baseball." *USA Today*, December 4, 1998.

Drebinger, John. "TV Fans See Catcher's Signals through Use of Special Camera; 80-Inch Lens in Center Field at Boston Shows Call for Pitchers—Device Spurs Sign Stealing Debate." *New York Times*, July 13, 1959.

Durslag, Melvin. "Secrets of the Sign Stealers." *Baseball Digest*, October 1953.

———. "When the Coach Rubs His Arm, Touches His Pants, Brushes His Wrist and Flicks His Ear . . . It's Really Very Simple: He Wants a Bunt." *TV Guide*, July 7, 1979.

Dyer, Braven. "Rig Raps Spy Charge Tossed at '59 Giants." *The Sporting News*, April 4, 1962.

Effrat, Louis. "Special Lens for Baseball TV Shuttered by Frick's Request." *New York Times*, July 14, 1959.

———. "Turley Conquers White Sox, 6 to 4; But Yankee Starter Needs Help from Morgan." *New York Times*, May 20, 1956.

Einstein, Charles, ed. *The Fireside Book of Baseball*. 3 vols. New York: Simon and Schuster, 1956, 1958, and 1968.

———. "Manager Uses a Decoy to Give Signals." *San Francisco Chronicle*, August 2, 1966.

Erskine, Carl. *Tales from the Dodger Dugout*. Champagne IL: Sports, 2000.

Evans, Billy. "Tipping the Signals." *Pearson's Magazine* (American edition), July 1914.

Evers, John J. "Stallings Will Show Up Mackmen: Capt. Evers Says Braves Will Go after Them from Start of World Series." *New York Times*, October 9, 1914.

Evers, John J., and Hugh S. Fullerton. *Touching Second: The Science of Baseball*. Chicago: Reilly & Britton, 1910.

Falls, Joe. "A Master at Sign Stealing." *Baseball Digest*, June 1999.

Finder, Chuck. "The Big Picture: Former Pirate Stole Signs for 1951 Giants." *Pittsburgh Post-Gazette*, July 9, 2001.

Finnigan, Bob. "Mariners Had More than a Few Zany Moments in Concrete Coffin." *Seattle Times*, June 22, 1999.

Fonseca, Lew. "Most Valuable Player . . . the Catcher." *Popular Mechanics*, June 1956.

Frank, Stanley. "Will They Steal This Series?" *Saturday Evening Post,*
October 2, 1937.

Fresco, Robert. "Joseph Reichler, 73, Baseball Writer and Hall of Famer."
Newsday, December 13, 1988.

Fullerton, Hugh S. "The Right and Wrong of Baseball: Tricks and
Schemes, Blocking and Interfering." *American Magazine,* October 1911.

———. "Watch His Arm! The Science of Coaching." *American Magazine,* August 1911.

Gammons, Peter. "Sign Language." *Sports Illustrated,* April 15, 1991.

Garagiola, Joe. "Signs of the Times." In *Sports All-Stars 1966, Baseball,*
edited by Harold Rosenthal. New York: Maco, 1966.

Gaven, Michael. "Thou Shalt Not Steal—Signs." *Baseball Digest,* May 1947.

Gerlach, Larry R. *The Men in Blue: Conversations with Umpires.* New
York: Viking Press, 1980.

Glier, Ray. "Put the Fun Back into Fundamentals." *USA Today Baseball
Weekly,* March 3, 1999.

Goddard, Joe. "Lost Art: Stealing Signs from Catcher." *The Sporting
News,* April 12, 1980.

———. "Stealing Signs from Second." *Baltimore Scorecard* (1980).

———. "Third Base Coaches: They Deal in Sign Language." *Baseball
Digest,* November 1978.

Goewey, Ed A. "Baseball Wig-Wagging." *Leslie's Illustrated Weekly,* May
18, 1918.

———. "Gossip and Pictures from the World of Sport." *Leslie's Illustrated Weekly,* July 1, 1909.

———. "The Old Fan: Inconsistency and Its Relation to Various Sports."
Leslie's Illustrated Weekly, August 11, 1910.

———. "The Old Fan Says." *Leslie's Illustrated Weekly,* September 11, 1913.

———. "Sporting Gossip from the Old Fan's Notebook." *Leslie's Illustrated Weekly,* February 24, 1910.

Goldberg, Hy. "Di-Jests." *Baseball Digest,* September 1947.

Golenbock, Peter. *Bums: An Oral History of the Brooklyn Dodgers.* New
York: Putnam's, 1984.

Grayson, Frank Y. "They Really Stole Signs Then." *Baseball Digest,*
August 1948.

Greenberg, Hank. *Hank Greenberg, the Story of My Life.* New York:
Times Books, 1989.

Gutman, Dan. *It Ain't Cheatin' If You Don't Get Caught.* New York: Pen-
guin, 1990.

Hagen, Paul. "Sign Stealing, It's Still Part of the Game." *Baseball Digest*, June 1979.

Hamill, Pete. *Snow in August*. New York: Little, Brown, 1997.

Hano, Arnold. "On the Diamond the Organization Man Calls Signals." *New York Times*, April 15, 1962.

Harwell, Ernie. *Ernie Harwell's Diamond Gems*. Ann Arbor MI: Momentum Books, 1991.

Hawkins, Burton. "Cookie Lavagetto's Signal Achievements." *Baseball Digest*, July 1958.

Heiling, Joe. "Signal-Stealing: A Dying Art?" *Baseball Digest*, December 1966.

Hemus, Solly. "The Crucial Art of Sign Stealing." In *1964 Baseball Guidebook*, edited by Harold Rosenthal. New York: Maco, 1964.

Henrich, Tommy, with A. L. Plaut. *The Way to Better Baseball: A Guide for Young Ball Players and Their Coaches*. New York: Exposition Press, 1971.

Hermann, Mark. "It's Sharp to Get an Edge." *Newsday*, February 1, 2001.

Hern, Gerry. "Old Camp Ground Visit Stir's Babe's Memories." *The Sporting News*, March 24, 1948.

Hernandez, Keith, and Mike Bryan. *Pure Baseball: Pitch by Pitch for the Advanced Fan*. New York: HarperCollins, 1994.

Hershiser, Orel. *Out of the Blue*. Brentwood TN: Wolgemuth & Hyatt, 1989.

Hertzel, Bob. "Cheating Frowned on, but Still a Part of Baseball." *Baseball Digest*, September 1984.

Hicks, C. B. "Baseball Sign Language." *Popular Mechanics*, April 1955, 142–45.

Holtzman, Jerome. "They're Stealing Leo's Signs." *The Sporting News*, July 8, 1972.

Holtzman, Jerry. "Cardinals Called Cardwell Tosses from Scoreboard." *The Sporting News*, May 17, 1961.

Honig, Donald. *The Man in the Dugout: Fifteen Big League Managers Speak Their Minds*. Lincoln: University of Nebraska Press, 1993.

Hornsby, Rogers. *My Kind of Baseball*. New York: McKay, 1953.

Hornsby, Rogers, and Bill Surface. *My War with Baseball*. New York: Coward-McCann, 1962.

——. "You've Got to Cheat to Win in Baseball." *True*, August 1961.

Isle, Stan. "Minors Pitch Inquiry of Pitch-Tipping." *The Sporting News*, October 17, 1981.

——. "Umps Reprimanded in Pitch-Tipping." *The Sporting News*, February 20, 1982.

Ivor-Campbell, Frederick. *Baseball's First Stars*. Cleveland OH: SABR, 1996.

Jacobson, Steve. "Revelation Still Doesn't Bring the '51 Pennant to Brooklyn." *Newsday*, February 1, 2001.

James, Bill. *The Baseball Book, 1991*. New York: Villard, 1991.

———. *The Bill James Guide to Baseball Managers from 1870 to Today*. New York: Scribner, 1997.

———. *The Bill James Historical Baseball Abstract*. New York: Villard, 1988.

Jennings, Tom. "Put Your Glasses Back On." *Baseball Research Journal* 20 (1991).

Katz, Fred. "Get Serious, Luke." *Sport*, August 1967.

———. "Hard to Be a Gentleman." *Sport*, July 1967.

Kavanaugh, Jack, and Norman Macht. *Uncle Robbie*. Cleveland OH: SABR, 1999.

Keidan, Bruce. "The Spies of Summer." *Sport*, April 1990.

Kelly, Kevin. "'Unwritten Rules' about Respect." *St. Petersburg (FL) Times*, August 12, 2001.

Kelly, Ray. "Foote's Feat Gives Phillies Big Kick." *The Sporting News*, September 23, 1978.

Kemp, Abe. "McCarthy's Signs Toughest: Vitt." *Baseball Digest*, August 1942.

Kenesson, Frank. "This Is How They Signal." *Baseball Digest*, June 1949.

Kerr, Kevin P. "The Signal Tipping Scam of 1909." *Baseball Research Journal* (1997).

Kiernan, Thomas. *The Miracle at Coogan's Bluff*. New York: Thomas Crowell, 1975.

King, Joe. "Zany Antics Flash Help Sign to Bull Pen." Signs and Signals file, National Baseball Library, n.d.

Kleinberg, Howard. "Rattling Baseball Skeletons." *Chattanooga (TN) Times*, February 18, 2001.

Knisley, Michael. "Mixed Signals." *The Sporting News*, June 2, 1997.

———. "Until This Season, Stealing Signs Was a Hidden Art." *The Sporting News*, May 2, 1997.

Koppett, Leonard. *The New Thinking Man's Guide to Baseball*. New York: Fireside Books, 1991.

Krout, John Allen. *Annals of American Sport*. New Haven CT: Yale University Press, 1929.

Kulfan, Ted. "Spying Players, Coaches Looking for Any Possible Advantage." *Detroit News*, June 5, 1997.

Kurkjian, Tim. "Sign Language." *Sports Illustrated*, July 27, 1997.

Lardner, John. "Quiet Larceny." *Newsweek*, May 12, 1941.

———. "Spies and Hangovers." *Newsweek*, September 28, 1953.

Lardner, Ring. *You Know Me Al*. 1914. Reprint, Cleveland OH: World, 1945.

Lebovitz, Hal. "'Built-In Radar' Helps Turley Swipe Signs." *The Sporting News*, November 17, 1962.

———. "The Indians Best Kept Secret." *Cleveland Plain Dealer*, May 31, 1981.

Leduff, Charlie. "A Telescopic Lens on a Baseball Legend." *New York Times*, February 9, 2001.

Levy, Sam. "City Slicker." *Baseball Digest*, May 1944.

Lewis, Allen. "Pickoff or Pitchout?" *Baseball Digest*, July 1978.

Lidz, Franz. "The Best Signs of the Times." *Sports Illustrated*, July 19, 1982.

Lieb, Frederick G. "Cloak-and-Dagger Men Nothing New, First Spies in '98." *The Sporting News*, July 13, 1960.

Light, Jonathan Frazer. *A Cultural Encyclopedia of Baseball*. Jefferson NC: McFarland, 1997.

Livingston, Bill, "'48 Team Proved Boys Will Be Boys." *Cleveland Plain Dealer*, July 1, 1998.

Lowitt, Bruce. "Larsen Brings Word 'Perfect' to Series." *St. Petersburg (FL) Times*, November 22, 1999.

Mack, Connie. *Connie Mack's Baseball Book*. New York: Alfred A. Knopf, 1950.

Mathewson, Christy. *Pitching in a Pinch; or, Baseball from the Inside*. New York: Putnam's, 1912.

Mays, Willie, with Howard Liss. *My Secrets of Playing Baseball*. New York: Viking Press, 1967.

McAfee, Skip. "Eloquence of Baseball Players." Paper presented at the annual meeting of the Society for American Baseball Research, Bob Davids Chapter, Baltimore, November 17, 2001.

McAuley, Ed. "Espionage in Cleveland." *Baseball Digest*, October 1954.

———. "O'Neill Ducks Tribe Row, but Spins Stories of Sign-Giving." *The Sporting News*, 1948.

———. "Sign-tific Discussion." *Baseball Digest*, February 1951.

———. "There's a Limit to Signs." *Baseball Digest*, August 1946.

McCue, Andy. "Baseball's Sign Language." *Riverside (CA) Press Enterprise*, March 30, 1989.

McDonald, Jack. "Signal Stealing Is an Overrated Trick." *San Francisco News Call Bulletin*, March 24, 1962.

———. "Spies Hurt Batters More than They Help—Haney." *The Sporting News*, April 4, 1962.

McDonough, Will. "Old-Timers, Ex-Players Recall the Thrill of the Cheat." *Boston Globe*, September 18, 1999.

McGuff, Joe. "A Way to Combat Pitch Stealing?" *Baseball Digest*, December 1957.

McQuay, Timothy. "Camera Shy." USA *Today Baseball Weekly*, May 7, 1997.

———. "Martinez Stealing Some Memories." USA *Today Baseball Weekly*, December 3, 1997.

Mead, William. *The Inside Game: Baseball's Master Strategists*. Alexandria VA: Redefinition, 1991.

Meany, Tom. "Lopez and the Indian Signs." *Collier's*, July 12, 1952.

———. "Tenth Man on a Ball Club." *Baseball Digest*, February 1943.

Mentus, Ron. "Sign Language: Baseball's Silent Strategy Code." *Baseball Digest*, September 1984.

Miller, Adam, and Tracy Connor. "Oldtimers Admit They Cheated on Da Bums." *New York Post*, February 1, 2001.

Minshew, Wayne. "Seeking the Winning Edge Is a Baseball Tradition." *Baseball Digest*, August 1978.

Monteleone, John J., ed. *Branch Rickey's Little Blue Book: Wit and Strategy from Baseball's Last Wise Man*. New York: Macmillan, 1995.

Morgan, Mark. "Talking Baseball: Irabu, Yanks Bridge Gap." CNN/SI *Online*, July 20, 1997.

Munzel, Edgar. "Birdie Spots Cub 'Sign-Swiper,' Wants Giles to Flash Red Light." *The Sporting News*, September 13, 1961.

———. "Tanner Gives Fans Credit for Rosy Record at Home." *The Sporting News*, September 9, 1972.

———. "Tepee 'Cub Scouts' Touch Off New Chi 'U-2' Turmoil." *The Sporting News*, July 13, 1960.

Murdock, Eugene. *Baseball Players and Their Times: Oral Histories of the Game, 1920–1940*. Westport CT: Meckler, 1991.

Murphy, Joe. "Recalling Baseball's Stolen Moments." *North Andover (MA) Eagle-Tribune*, February 24, 2001.

Mushnick, Phil. "Branca, Thomson Still in There Singin.'" *New York Post*, Sports section, January 25, 2001.

Muskat, Carrie. *Banks to Sandberg to Grace: Five Decades of Love and Frustration with the Chicago Cubs*. Chicago: Contemporary Books, 2001.

Nash, Bruce, and Allan Zullo. *The Baseball Hall of Shame*. New York: Pocket Books, 1985.

Newhan, Ross. "Some of Baseball's Best Thieves Have Done a Peach of a Job; Gamesmanship: For Charlton's Edification, Sign Stealing Has

Been Going on Forever and Is Part of the Lore of the Game." *Los Angeles Times*, September 12, 1991.

New York Times. "Chuck Dressen, Fiery Manager of Tigers, Dies." September 11, 1966.

Nightengale, Bob. "Arizona Video Man Turns into a Real Steal." *USA Today Baseball Weekly*, April 1, 1998.

Nightingale, Dave. "Baseball's Sign Language: Welcome to the Wild and Wonderful World of 'Indicators' and 'Activators.'" *The Sporting News*, March 5, 1984.

———. "Concentration Is Key to Code-Breaking." *The Sporting News*, March 5, 1984.

———. "Sox Keep Eye Out for Indians' Spy." *Chicago Daily News*, August 20, 1971.

O'Connor, Ian. "Branca-Thomson Bond as Strong as in 1951." *USA Today*, September 28, 2001.

O'Keeffe, Michael. "The Giants Stole the Pennant; 1951 Club Intercepted Signs." *New York Daily News*, February 1, 2001.

Okrant, Daniel. *Nine Innings*. New York: Ticknor & Fields, 1985.

Okrant, Daniel, and Harris Lewine. *The Ultimate Baseball Book*. Boston: Houghton Mifflin, 1984.

Olney, Buster. "Did Pettitte Tip Pitches?" *New York Times*, November 5, 2001.

———. "Is Irabu Tipping Pitches?" *New York Times*, June 27, 1998.

———. "Jeter Works on Defense as Shoulder Improves." *New York Times*, March 5, 2001.

———. "Signs to Batters: They're Part Art and Part Con." *Baseball Digest*, December 1993.

———. "Yankees Causing Havoc on the Bases." *New York Times*, May 8, 2001.

———. "Yanks First in East with Defeat of Baltimore." *New York Times*, July 4, 2001.

Orem, Preston. *Baseball from 1845 to 1881, from the Newspaper Accounts*. Altadena CA: self-published, 1961.

Oremland, Barbara. "The Silent World of Dummy Hoy." In *A Celebration of Louisville Baseball in the Major and Minor Leagues*. Cleveland OH: SABR, 1997.

Patton, Maurice. "Look Who's Not Talking: Signals Speak Louder than Words When It Comes to Playing Game." *Nashville Tennessean*, May 23, 2000.

Peebles, Dick. "Afraid of the Steal Sign!" *Baseball Digest*, March 1965.

Petrak, Cliff. *The Art and Science of Aggressive Baserunning*. Englewood Cliffs NJ: Prentice Hall, 1986.

Petroff, Tom. *Baseball Signs and Signals*. Dallas: Taylor, 1986.

Pfeffer, N. Fred. *Scientific Ball*. Chicago: N. Fred Pfeffer, 1889.

Phelon, William A. "Framing Up New Set of Baseball Signals." *Baseball Magazine*, April 1922.

Piersall, Jimmie. "How the Home Team Cheats." *Baseball Magazine*, May 1962.

Powers, Jimmy. "Stealing World Series Signs and Signals; There Are Spies in Baseball, Very Clever at Foretelling Plays. Here Are Inside Tips on the Art." *Liberty*, September 9, 1939.

Prager, Joshua. *The Echoing Green: The Untold Story of Bobby Thomson, Ralph Branca, and the Shot Heard Round the World*. New York: Pantheon, 2006.

Prager, Joshua Harris. "Was the '51 Giants Comeback a Miracle, or Did They Simply Steal the Pennant?" *Wall Street Journal*, January 31, 2001.

Pricbc, Brian. "99 Signing on (and Ways and Means of Running an Aggressive Offense from the Coaching Box and Dugout)." *Coach and Athletic Director Magazine*, January 1997.

Prince, Carl E. *Brooklyn's Dodgers: The Bums, the Borough, and the Best of Baseball, 1941–1957*. New York: Oxford University Press, 1996.

Rains, Rob. "Lefty's Not Tipping Hand on Hall Pitch." USA *Today Baseball Weekly*, July 27, 1994.

Reeder, Colonel Red. "Old Letter Credits Army Officer with Introducing Umpire's Signal." *The Sporting News*, April 11, 1970.

Reichler, Joe. *The Game and the Glory*. Englewood Cliffs NJ: Prentice Hall, 1976.

———. "Sign-Steal with Binoculars Set Up Thomson's Flag Winning Homer." Associated Press. *Washington Post*, March 23, 1967.

Reiter, Ben. *Astroball: The New Way to Win It All*. New York: Crown Archetype, 2018.

Richards, Paul. *Modern Baseball Strategy*. Englewood Cliffs NJ: Prentice Hall, 1955.

Ritter, Lawrence S. *The Glory of Their Times*. New York: Macmillan, 1966.

Roberts, Russell. *Stolen! A History of Base Stealing*. Jefferson NC: McFarland, 1999.

Robinson, Ray. *The Home Run Heard 'Round the World: The Dramatic Story of the 1951 Giants-Dodgers Pennant Race*. New York: HarperCollins, 1991.

Rosenfeld, Harvey. *The Great Chase: The Dodgers-Giants Pennant Race of 1951.* Jefferson NC: McFarland, 1992.

Rosenthal, Harold, ed. *1964 Baseball Guidebook.* New York: Maco, 1964.

——, ed. *Sports All-Stars 1966 Baseball.* New York: Maco, 1966.

Rumill, Ed. "On Stealing Signs and Swiping Signals." *Baseball Magazine,* February 1944.

——. "Umpiring Teamwork Improves Officiating." *Baseball Digest,* February 1966.

Russell, Fred. *Funny Thing about Sports.* Nashville: McQuiddy Press, 1948.

——. "How Stengel Handles Sign-Stealers." *Baseball Digest,* June 1959.

Safire, William. *Quoth the Mavin.* New York: Random House, 1993.

Salisbury, Jim. "Scouts See That Yanks Succeed." *Santa Rosa (CA) Press Democrat,* October 24, 2001.

Salsinger, H. G. "Connie Originated Signals." *Baseball Digest,* June 1954.

Sangree, Allen. "The Strategy of Baseball." *Everybody's Magazine* 15 (1906).

Schechter, Leonard. "The Fiend with Glasses." Reprinted in *The Best Sports Stories of 1963.* New York: E. P. Dutton, 1964.

Schneider, Russell. *The Boys of the Summer of '48.* Champaign IL: Sports, 1998.

Schuessler, Raymond. "Accusers Right—Tribe Had a Spy in Bleachers." *The Sporting News,* July 22, 1972.

Sherwin, Bob. "Mariners Squeeze Out a Victory over Detroit." *Seattle Times,* June 18, 1999.

Shirley, Bill. "Why Doesn't Good Defense Get More Recognition?" *Baseball Digest,* December 1984.

Smelser, Marshall. *The Life That Ruth Built.* New York: Quadrangle, 1985.

Smith, Curt. *What Baseball Means to Me.* New York: Warner Books, 2002.

Smith, David. "Play by Play Analysis of the 1951 National League Pennant Race." Presentation at the Society for American Baseball Research Convention, Milwaukee, July 12, 2001.

Smith, Ira, and H. Allen Smith. *Low and Inside.* New York: McGraw-Hill, 1947.

Smith, Lyall. "Signing Off." *Baseball Digest,* July 1949.

Smith, Red. "A Curve in the Clutch: Frisch Recalls 1934 Pennant Payoff Pitch." *Baseball Digest,* June 1954.

Southworth, Harold S. *The Complete Book of Baseball Signs and Plays.* Champaign IL: Sagamore, 1999.

Spackman, Robert R. *Baseball.* Annapolis: United States Naval Institute, 1963.

The Sporting News. "Braves Hope for Big Inning Shattered in Signal Mixup." May 4, 1960.

————. "Conlan Tells Brave Bull-Pen Crew to Land: U-2 Incident?" June 15, 1960.

————. "Mauch Has Idea Chuck Still Up to Signal-Stealing Habit." May 11, 1960.

————. "McCarthy Kept Signs Simple, Had No Teamwork Problems." July 13, 1960.

————. "O'Toole Fouled Up 3 Signs in Turning Back Phils, 1-0." May 25, 1960.

————. "Say It Ain't So, Cholly." July 13, 1960.

————. "Stealing Signs Complicated; Too Many Types of Pitches." July 13, 1960.

————. "Too Many Signals Burden Batters Today, Cobb Feels." February 20, 1957.

Sports Illustrated. "The Camera Catches a Thief: The Wonderful World of Sport." July 15, 1957.

————. "I Spy." June 15, 1970.

————. "Signals and Spies, Signals and Spies." July 2, 1956.

————. "Signs and Science." July 27, 1959.

————. "Spy Story." July 18, 1960.

Stockton, J. Roy. "Five Signs to Success." *Baseball Digest*, February 1952.

Stout, Glenn. *Yankees Century: One Hundred Years of New York Yankee Baseball.* Boston: Houghton Mifflin, 2002.

Stump, Al. *Cobb: A Biography.* Chapel Hill NC: Algonquin Books, 1994.

Surface, Bill. "Last Days of Rogers Hornsby." *Saturday Evening Post*, June 15, 1963.

Taylor, Sec. "The Inside on Outside Signs." *Baseball Digest*, October 1961.

Tebbetts, Birdie. "I'd Rather Catch." *Atlantic Monthly*, September 1949.

Thomson, Bobby. *The Giants Win the Pennant!* New York: Kensington, 1991.

Thrift, Syd. *The Game according to Syd: The Theories and Teachings of Baseball's Leading Innovator.* New York: Simon and Schuster, 1990.

Topkin, Marc. "First Blow to M's." *St. Petersburg (FL) Times*, October 4, 2000.

USA Today Baseball Weekly. Cleveland Indians. June 10, 1998.

————. Montreal Expos. May 14, 1997.

————. "Oh, What a Scandal!" December 9, 1998.

————. Philadelphia Phillies. September 24, 1997.

Veech, Ellis J. "When the Bunt Sign Is Flashed." *Baseball Magazine*, July 1947.

Veeck, Bill. *Veeck—as in Wreck*. New York: Putnam's, 1962.

Visser, Lesley. "A Bit Difficult to Explain." *Boston Globe*, May 3, 1981.

Vogel, O. H. *Ins and Outs of Baseball*. St. Louis: C. V. Mosby, 1952.

Waldstein, David. "Giants Won the Pennant, but They Stole the Signals." *Newark (NJ) Star-Ledger*, February 1, 2001.

Walfoort, Cleon. "Mates Didn't Talk to Cobb—So Jones Relayed Signals." *The Sporting News*, July 26, 1961.

———. "Most 'Signs' by Coaches Merely Camouflage." *Baseball Digest*, December 1960.

Ward, John Montgomery. *Base-Ball: How to Become a Player*. 1888. Reprint, Cleveland OH: SABR, 1993.

Wendel, Tim. "ALCS Woes Give McDowell Reputation as a Big Tipper." *USA Today Baseball Weekly*, November 17, 1993.

Werber, Bill, and C. Paul Rogers III. *Memories of a Ballplayer*. Cleveland OH: SABR, 2001.

White, Paul. "Giants Stole the Pennant? Perhaps Not." *USA Today Baseball Weekly*, March 21, 2001.

———. "Let's Let the Umpire Assignment Secret Out." *USA Today Baseball Weekly*, October 14, 1998.

———. "Why Is Peeking Such a Sin?" *USA Today Baseball Weekly*, June 16, 1993.

Will, George. *Men at Work*. New York Macmillan, 1990.

———. "A Season Spoiled." *Washington Post*, February 8, 2001.

Williams, Pete. "Back to Basics in Swings, Signs." *USA Today Baseball Weekly*, August 19, 1992.

Wolf, Bob. "Did Giants Swipe Signals? 'Ridiculous,' Dark Declares." *The Sporting News*, May 10, 1961.

Wood, Hal. "How Tigers Stole 1940 Flag." *Baseball Digest*, April 1949.

Woods, David. *A History of Tactical Communication Techniques*. Orlando: Orlando Division, Martin, Martin-Marietta, 1965.

Wray, J. Edward. *How to Run the Bases*. New York: American Sports, 1915.

Young, Dick. "The Great Spy Controversy." *The Sporting News*, October 18, 1976.

———. "Vas You Effer a Spy in Milwaukee?" *The Sporting News*, July 10, 1975.

Ziegel, Vic. "About Time We Gave This Story a Rest." *New York Daily News*, February 11, 2001.

INDEX

Kling, John, 45–46, 160n3
Knight, Ray, 96
Konikowski, Alex, 84
Koppett, Leonard, 108
Koufax, Sandy, 91–92
Kubek, Tony, 91
Kurkjian, Tim, 134

Labine, Clem, 83
Landis, Kenesaw Mountain, 138
Lardner, John, 71
Larsen, Don, 73
LaRussa, Tony, 5, 102, 132
Latham, Arlie, 50, 138
Lawrence, Brooks, 81
Lawson, Roxie, 70
Lee, Don, 88
Lehrback, Phil, xiii
Lemon, Bob, 66
Leppert, Don, 141
Live Ball Era, 54, 56–69, 162n1
Lockman, Whitey, 82, 106
Lopez, Andy, 143
Los Angeles Angels, 88, 119
Los Angeles Dodgers, 11, 95
Louisville American Association
    team, 27
Luderus, Fred, 57
Luhnow, Jeff, 113

Mack, Connie, 8, 13, 25, 26, 29, 40,
    45–53, 60, 67, 130, 160–61n5
MacPhail, Larry, 61
Maddon, Joe, 119
Maglie, Sal "The Barber," 67
Major League Baseball, 77, 111–12
Manfred, Fred, 116–17, 123
Mann, Jack, 103
Mantle, Mickey, 91

Marion, Marty, 85
Maris, Roger, 80, 91, 169–70n14
Marquard, Rube, 47–48, 59
Martin, Billy, 71, 93
Martinez, Dave, 118
Mathews, Eddie, 69, 171n3
Mathewson, Christy, 14, 45–46,
    47–48, 109, 139, 159–60n15
Mattingly, Don, 97
Mauch, Gene, 76, 85, 91, 95, 172n10
Mays, Carl, 56–57
Mays, Willie, 83, 91
McCann, Gene, 40
McCarthy, Joe, 57–58, 60, 146
McCue, Andy, 95
McDonald, Arch, xiii
McDonald, Jack, 85
McGowan, Bill, 36
McGraw, John, 27, 29, 42, 51–53,
    157n25
McKeon, Jack, 132–33
McLemore, Mark, 11
Mead, Bill, 128
Meany, Tom, 70
Medwick, Joe, 65
Merkle, Fred, 42, 159–60n15
Metheny, Bud, xv
Metro, Charlie, 92–93
Meyers, Chief, 47–50
Michaels, Ed, 7
Miller, Ray, 6
Mills, A. G., 21
Milwaukee Braves, 75, 77, 86, 92
Milwaukee Brewers, 14, 90
Minneapolis Millers, 61
"The Miracle of Coogan's Bluff,"
    15, 82, 103, 106
The Miracle of Coogan's Bluff
    (Kiernan), 106